The Battle of Gloucester
1777

SMALL BATTLES

Mark Edward Lender and James Kirby Martin, Series Editors

The Battles of Connecticut Farms and Springfield, 1780
by Edward G. Lengel

The Battle of Harlem Heights, 1776
by David Price

The Battle of Musgrove's Mill, 1780
by John Buchanan

The Battle OF Gloucester

1777

GARRY WHEELER STONE

AND

PAUL W. SCHOPP

SMALL BATTLES

WESTHOLME
Yardley

Westholme Publishing, LLC
904 Edgewood Road
Yardley, Pennsylvania 19067
Visit our Web site at www.westholmepublishing.com

ISBN: 978-1-59416-384-5
Also available as an eBook.

Printed in the United States of America.

For Barclay, Graham, Rosa, and Julian
GWS

To the memory of the local historians who taught and inspired me: David C. Munn, William R. Farr, and William W. Leap
PWS

Contents

Maps

A gallery of illustrations follows page 48

Series Editors' Introduction

WE ALL HAVE HEARD and likely read about the big battles of the American Revolution. Names like Trenton, Saratoga, and Yorktown resonate in our ears. But what about all the smaller battles that took place by the hundreds, often fought away from but related to the bigger battles. It is the contention of this series that these smaller actions, too often ignored, had as much impact, if not more, in shaping the outcomes of the American War of Independence.

These engagements were most often fought at the grassroots level. They did not directly involve His Majesty's professional forces under the likes of Generals William Howe, John Burgoyne, and Henry Clinton, or Continentals under Generals George Washington, Nathanael Greene, or Horatio Gates for that matter. Such smaller battles involved local forces, such as patriot militia and partisan bands of Loyalists, or at times Native Americans mostly, but not always, fighting on the British side.

Quite often the big names were not there in such smaller-scale combat. Private Joseph Plumb Martin, writing in his classic memoir, recalled his fighting at Forts Mifflin and Mercer during November 1777. He and his comrades were trying to block British war and supply vessels moving up the Delaware River from reaching the king's troops under Sir William Howe who had captured Philadelphia. Had they prevailed and cut off this obvious supply route, Howe might well had had to abandon the city. But no, they did not succeed. Superior British firepower finally defeated these courageous American fighters.

What bothered Martin, besides so many good soldiers being seriously wounded or killed, was not the failed but valiant effort to cut off Howe's primary supply line. Rather, writing thirty years later, what particularly irked him was that "there has been but little notice taken of" this critical action. Martin was sure he knew why: "The reason of which is, there was no Washington, Putnam, or Wayne there. . . . Such [circumstances] and such troops generally get but little notice taken of them, do what they will. Great men get great praise, little men, nothing."

While Martin's blunt lament is unusual in the literature of the Revolution, the circumstances he described and complained of are actually fairly obvious. Although often brutal, the smaller engagements too frequently have received short shrift in popular narratives about the conflict. Nor have the consequences of these various actions been carefully studied in relation to the bigger battles and the outcomes of the War for Independence more generally. Small battles accounted for the lion's share of the combat that occurred during the American Revolution. The purpose of this series is to shine a bright new light on these smaller engagements while also getting to know those lesser persons who participated in them and grappling with the broader consequences and greater meaning of these actions on local, regional, and nation-making levels.

In the end, a more complete understanding of the Revolutionary War's big picture will emerge from the small-battles volumes that make up this series. If, as recent scholarship tells us, local history "allows us to peer deep into past societies and to see their very DNA," the Small Battles Series will do the same for the American War of Independence.

Thus, we are very pleased to bring your attention to *The Battle of Gloucester, 1777,* by Garry Wheeler Stone and Paul W. Schopp.

Both authors are recognized authorities on the Revolutionary War and its historical and archaeological record in the Delaware River Valley and southern New Jersey. They have traced the course of the battle—actually a running skirmish of some forty-five minutes' duration—fought in Gloucester, New Jersey, on November 25, 1777. The fighting drew in New Jersey militia, a contingent of Continental riflemen, and Hessian jagers—the elite German light infantry. Significantly, the battle saw the marquis de Lafayette in his first combat command, and Stone and Schopp argue persuasively that his performance was enough to convince Washington and other rebel authorities that the young Frenchman was ready for a senior Continental command—a development with profound implications for the revolutionary cause. Seldom has a small battle produced such important results, and *The Battle of Gloucester, 1777* is now the most telling account we have of this brief but genuinely important engagement.

Mark Edward Lender
James Kirby Martin
Series editors

Introduction

A REVOLUTIONARY WAR ICON was born on November 25, 1777. That afternoon, the twenty-year-old marquis de Lafayette led three hundred to four hundred Americans in an attack on a Hessian outpost in Gloucester County, New Jersey.* The Americans routed and drove the Hessians back almost two and a half miles onto the enemy's main body under Charles, 2nd Earl Cornwallis. The marquis's successful attack yielded the only good news in a failed American effort to maintain a blockade of the Delaware River, intended to starve the British out of Philadelphia. The sharp skirmish—known as the Battle of Gloucester—was a little victory that produced dramatic results. It provided Lafayette with his first command experience, and Commander in Chief George Washington used the victory to convince Congress that the young man was ready for bigger things. The delegates agreed to Lafayette taking command of a Continental army division, an opportunity the Frenchman had hungered for since his arrival in

---

*Gloucester was a county, a township (the Town of Gloucester, or Gloucestertown Township), and a hamlet "Gloucester Town."

America. It was instrumental in committing him to the cause of American independence, an event with major implications for the outcome of the revolutionary struggle.

But why was a wealthy French aristocrat in America? Who was this man? In 1757, Gilbert du Motier, the future marquis, was born in south-central France in the Chateau of Chavaniac. The child inherited a martial lineage, but luck did not always accompany courage. A month before Gilbert's second birthday, on August 1, 1759, his father, the marquis de Lafayette, died fighting an Anglo-German army at the Battle of Minden. Shortly thereafter, Gilbert's mother left the chateau's mountain valley to live with her father and grandfather in Paris. Left alone, the young marquis remained at Chavaniac, where his grandmother and two aunts raised him, along with a girl cousin as a playmate. The Chavaniac women instilled within him a strong moral compass, but he lacked male role models. At eleven, his guardians dispatched Lafayette, a shy country bumpkin, to Paris to live with his mother and great-grandfather. Enrolled in excellent schools, Gilbert became a nominal member of the king's body guards, the Black Musketeers. In 1773, his future father-in-law, the duc d'Ayen, arranged a commission for Lafayette in the family's dragoon regiment, commanded by the duc's son, Philippe Louis, prince de Poix. The following April, Lafayette married the duc's daughter Adrienne. By this time, three inheritances had made the young man immensely wealthy. Despite his wealth, however, he felt uncomfortable in the royal society where his marriage placed him. Beneath the silence lay a very bright, intensely ambitious young man, determined not to become a mere courtier.[1]

During summer 1775, the Noailles Dragoons and Captain Lafayette traveled to Metz for training. Lieutenant General Charles-François, comte de Broglie, the younger brother of maréchal Victor-François, duc de Broglie, one of France's most successful generals of the Seven Years' War, commanded the garrison. Also at Metz, called up out of retirement, was Lieutenant Colonel Baron de Kalb, one of the Broglie brothers' favorite subordinates.

On August 8, comte de Broglie invited dragoon captain Lafayette to dinner. The guest of honor at the dinner was a distinguished English visitor, Prince William Henry, Duke of Gloucester, a younger brother of George III. Gloucester was a Whig, and Broglie was eager to weaken Britain—and perhaps create an opportunity for himself—and discussion of the growing revolt in America flowed freely. Unknown to Lafayette, the comte de Broglie had a grandiose agenda. He wanted to pack the Continental army with French officers, replace Washington as commander in chief, and after successful campaigns against the English, be elected president for life, the equivalent of the Dutch *stadtholder*. For the comte de Broglie, the idea of a general from one country commanding troops in another would not have seemed strange. An Englishman, the Duke of Marlborough, had commanded allied British, Dutch, and Austrian troops in the campaigns in the Germanys and Spanish Netherlands. The idea gained traction among the Continental Congress's agents in Paris, but the comte's agent, Baron de Kalb—after arriving in America—quickly realized that the idea was "totally impractical."[2]

De Broglie would do more to cultivate Captain Lafayette. De Broglie was a Mason, and he sponsored the young captain's entrance into the secret society. On December 15, 1775, Lafayette became a member of the Saint John of Scotland of the Social Contract lodge in Paris. Within masonic lodges, members enjoyed fellowship and recreation combined with lectures on science. Whatever their ethnicity, religion, or social rank, the society considered all Masons brothers, working for the betterment of mankind. Masonic precepts become obvious in Lafayette's life, but of more immediate benefit to the young man was his joining an international fraternity that included many influential Americans and French. Some of the masons who became important to Lafayette were George Washington, Benjamin Franklin, Henry Laurens, and the comte de Rochambeau.[3]

The comte de Broglie's attention to Lafayette in 1775 probably had nothing to do with his aspirations to become an American *stadtholder* (to go to America, Broglie wanted "not courtiers, but excellent and well-tried soldiers").[4] Broglie also sponsored the entrance of Lafayette's younger brother-in-law, Louis-Marie, vicomte de Noailles, into masonry. Madame Lafayette's father, once a former army officer, became a famous chemist; her grandfather, the duc de Noailles, was a maréchal of France; and her older brother, the prince de Poix, commanded the Noailles Dragoon Regiment in which Lafayette served. A favor done for the duc's family today might be reciprocated in the future. Neither the comte de Broglie nor the young marquis could anticipate how soon they would need each other's help.[5]

In August 1775, Lafayette may have enjoyed listening to the Duke of Gloucester and the comte discuss the growing revolt in America, but it held little relevance to him. Lafayette already had a path to honor, as had his father, in the French army under the friendly tutelage of the comte de Broglie. Should the marquis's brother-in-law be promoted, Lafayette could anticipate purchasing command of the Noailles Dragoons. Then, in June 1776, that path disappeared. A new minister of war reformed the French army and placed surplus officers, including Lafayette, in reserve status, disheartening the eighteen-year-old marquis. How would he make a name for himself? How could he be as brave as his father? That fall, Lafayette and two of his friends, Louis-Marie, vicomte de Noailles (his youngest brother-in-law) and Louis-Philippe, comte de Ségur (the son of a future minister of war), learned that French officers planned to sail for America and fight against England. When the vicomte applied to his uncle, the duc d'Ayen, for help in obtaining permission to go to America, the duc refused. Louis-Marie and Louis-Philippe abandoned the idea, but the disappointed Lafayette applied for help to the comte de Broglie. With some misgivings, the comte introduced the marquis to the Baron de Kalb.[6]

Lieutenant Colonel Johann de Kalb had been assistant quartermaster general for the Broglies. He had served so well in staff and field that in 1763, he was awarded the Order of Military Merit. In fall 1776, he reentered active service, was made a brigadier general for the French West Indies, and then was immediately furloughed for two years "to go abroad in order to look after his personal business"—in other words, the French Ministry of War had approved comte de Broglie's plan to pack the Continental army with French officers. De Kalb proved an excellent choice to implement the plan while Broglie remained in the background. The colonel remained loyal to the comte, spoke English, and in 1768 had traveled in America, gathering intelligence for the French foreign minister.[7]

De Kalb recruited officers eager to go to America. After Broglie introduced de Kalb to the Continental Congress's agent in Paris, Silas Deane, on November 5, 1776, de Kalb began bringing them to meet Deane. On December 6, Deane forwarded to Congress a list of sixteen officers to serve in the Continental forces. De Kalb and Deane had not included Lafayette on this list, but de Kalb had met with the young man several times in November. On December 7, de Kalb returned to Deane with Lafayette at his side, and that day Lafayette gained his wish—a contract to serve in the Continental army. Deane promised Lafayette the rank of major general due to "his high Birth, his Alliances, the great Dignities which his Family holds at this Court, [. . .] and above all his Zeal for the Liberty of our Provinces." In signing, the marquis added that he would serve without pay or "allowance."[8]

De Kalb planned to sail in early December, but the Continental army's defeat at Long Island, the indiscretion of officers planning to go to America, and the English ambassador's vigorous protests forced the French government to halt departures to the United States. Any expedition to America would occur in secret, without any support from the French government or the American agents in Paris.[9]

In February 1777, the nineteen-year-old marquis's wealth came to his rescue. Afraid that Broglie's plans would fail, Broglie's secretary persuaded Lafayette to purchase a ship to carry Baron de Kalb's group of officers to America. In the middle of February, Lafayette bought a ship, but the following two months proved stressful for him. His family, furious with the marquis, tried to prevent his departure. On April 20, 1777, however, Lafayette's ship, *La Victoire*, sailed for America with the marquis, de Kalb, thirteen other French officers, and an American named Edmund Brice onboard. Brice was the younger brother of wealthy Maryland lawyers and landowners. He was studying art in London when William Carmichael, secretary to American agent Deane, recruited him to accompany Lafayette. Three of the passengers on *La Victoire* would become part of Lafayette's staff for the next several years. Brice and Jean-Joseph Sourbader de Gimat, a French army lieutenant, would be his aides-de-camp, commissioned in August as Continental army majors. Michel Capitaine du Chesnoy would eventually be commissioned a captain in the Continental army's corps of engineers and would map the marquis's battles. Lafayette spent part of the fifty-six-day voyage studying English with Baron de Kalb and Brice.[10]

If the voyage to America proved tedious, the landing at Charleston, South Carolina, difficult, the trip overland to Philadelphia was hideous. Carriages disintegrated, horses died, and some party members fell ill. The first passengers from *La Victoire* did not reach Philadelphia until July 27. And the worst was yet to come. The members of the Continental Congress did not want them. Their agent in Paris, Silas Deane, had flooded them with French officers. Twenty-two had landed April 22 at Portsmouth, New Hampshire, with artillerist Philippe Charles Tronson du Coudray, while four more concomitantly arrived at Boston. Some brought needed skills, others obnoxious manners. American officers objected to foreigners displacing them. The Continental Congress was struggling to cope with the influx of Europeans when Lafayette's group arrived in Philadelphia. Only the English-speaking de Kalb—remembered from his 1768 trip to America—and Lafayette received a warm welcome. De Kalb, a mature, experienced officer, received a major general's commission in September.[11]

The nineteen-year-old marquis received his commission earlier. On July 31, 1777, only days after his arrival in the de facto rebel capital, Congress commissioned Lafayette a major general in the

Continental army—making the marquis the youngest individual to hold the rank in American military history. The commission came "in consideration of his zeal, illustrious family and connexions"[12] (paraphrasing Deane's language in Lafayette's contract). The delegates, however, were not about to trust a teenager with an actual command—much less the command of a division, the usual assignment for a major general. The commission came with an understanding that the inexperienced French youth's rank was honorary, although from courtesy his commission did not contain such language. Lafayette would lead no troops, a concept understood by Congress and the officer corps—but not accepted by Lafayette. The marquis was not happy. He wanted battlefield responsibility and, like so many officers of the period, military glory. To gain an opportunity, he had left a beautiful wife, spent a small fortune, angered his family, and annoyed his sovereign. Biding his time, he would await his chance; meanwhile, he would have to be content with an attachment to Washington's headquarters.[13]

Lafayette had joined the rebel army at a critical juncture. After a promising start in early 1777, the fortunes of war were about to turn against the Continental army and its commander in chief, George Washington. On August 25, 1777, an Anglo-German army of more than 16,498 men under General Sir William Howe had landed at the head of Chesapeake Bay.[14] Thus began a sequence of British victories and American embarrassments. Howe's troops brushed aside rebel opposition at Cooch's Bridge in Delaware; outmaneuvered and outfought the Continental army at Brandywine Creek in Pennsylvania; outmaneuvered Washington at the Schuylkill River fords; and, on September 26, marched unopposed into Philadelphia. Now the largest city in British North America and the capital of the Revolution was in the hands of the enemy. On October 4, Washington surprised the British with an all-out counterattack on their encampment at the Philadelphia suburb of Germantown. The Continentals gave the British a scare—Howe would order reinforcements sent to him from the New York garrison—but at the end of the day, the British beat back the Continentals. For Washington it was a bitter defeat.

After Germantown, the British withdrew into Philadelphia. While they felt safe behind their redoubts, they remained isolated. The Pennsylvania Committee of Safety had spent enormous sums fortifying the port of Philadelphia. It had constructed and manned a riverine navy, strengthened Fort Mifflin (on Mud Island on the Pennsylvania side of the Delaware River), constructed two additional forts on the New Jersey shore (at Billingsport and Red Bank), and narrowed the shipping channel with underwater, iron-tipped obstacles (*chevaux-de-Frise*). These measures effectively denied the British the use of the Delaware as a supply route. In addition, Pennsylvania and New Jersey had outlawed trade with the enemy. Militia and detachments from the Continental army enforced this embargo.

For General Howe, the situation was critical. To supply his army and feed Philadelphia's civilians, the British had to send heavily guarded convoys overland from Chester, the farthest point upriver the Royal Navy could safely venture. A trickle of supplies also reached the city via riverine small craft, sneaking up the Delaware under cover of darkness. If the river remained blocked until it froze over, as it generally did, it would make Howe's supply problems impossible and his hold on Philadelphia unsustainable.

Fortunately for Howe, hard fighting and rebel miscalculations finally opened the Delaware for the Royal Navy. Washington and his generals had inspected Philadelphia's port defenses in August 1777. The very competent French artillerist and engineer Du Coudray (now a Continental army major general), had charge of completing the river defenses. Du Coudray and Brigadier Generals Henry Knox and Anthony Wayne recommended improving the fortifications of Billingsport and garrisoning the post. They also wanted to strongly hold Fort Mifflin and Red Bank (later named Fort Mercer). Major General Nathanael Greene, still smarting from the loss of Fort Washington, advocated only garrisoning Fort Mifflin while defending the chevaux-de-Frise and the Jersey shore with infantry and 18-pounder guns on traveling carriages. Washington, however, chose to ignore their advice. Instead, he fixated on keeping his army intact to defeat the enemy in the field. "Except General Howe can be checked upon land," he insisted, "the obstructions in the River will be of little avail."[15] Hence, he refused to garrison the fort at Billingsport and acted almost too late in garrisoning Forts Mifflin and Mercer.

Washington relented and garrisoned Mifflin and Mercer only after his repulse at Germantown made clear that defeating Howe in open battle was unlikely. The subsequent defense of the Delaware forts proved bloody and drawn out. On October 22, rebels at Fort Mercer smashed a Hessian attack, inflicting hideous casualties on the Germans, but it only provided a respite. The night of November 15–16, after an epic defense of thirty-seven days, Fort Mifflin's garrison evacuated the ruins of the fort. Only Fort Mercer now prevented British supply ships from reaching Philadelphia wharves. Washington sent relief to Mercer, but he acted too late. On November 20–21, as Cornwallis threatened with 4,250 men, Fort Mercer's garrison evacuated, and the Pennsylvania navy burned much of its fleet. The port of Philadelphia now stood open to British shipping, and Washington had lost his opportunity to starve the British out of the city. However, Washington's decision to keep his forces consolidated did allow him to confine the enemy to Philadelphia. On December 4, when Howe ventured out to attack the Continental army camp at Whitemarsh, he failed to draw Washington into a major fight, and after three days of skirmishing, he returned to Philadelphia. The fighting in New Jersey, however, was not over—and Lafayette was about to get his chance.

WHILE HE HAD HELD NO COMMAND, the Frenchman was no stranger to combat. At the Battle of Brandywine, September 11, 1777, the marquis dismounted and joined the troops of Brigadier Thomas Conway's brigade. While Lafayette was trying to steady the men, a musket ball struck his lower leg. Major Gimat helped him remount his horse, and, hastily bandaged, Lafayette continued to rally troops until nightfall. Then he was evacuated to Philadelphia, and later to the Moravian hospital at Bethlehem.[16]

The marquis only rejoined the Continental army on October 19, 1777. During this period, the British actively sought to reduce the rebel forts that controlled the river approaches to Philadelphia. Lafayette eagerly waited for another chance to prove himself, and it came on November 19, when Washington ordered Major General Greene to lead 3,100 Continentals to New Jersey to relieve Fort Mercer. The marquis asked to go along, and Greene happily agreed, the next evening writing his wife of Lafayette's "noble enthusiasm" for the cause of liberty and saying he "is a most sweet temperd young gentleman." They arrived too late, only crossing the Delaware River into New Jersey on November 21. After General John Glover's brigade joined the force, Greene advanced on the British, hoping to attack Cornwallis. On November 26, however, when Greene arrived in Haddonfield, he learned that the British held a strong position on the Gloucester Town peninsula, where Royal Navy artillery protected the flanks. None of Greene's brigadiers advised attacking; the Continentals had now lost any chance of recapturing Philadelphia.[17]

Yet the young marquis—he turned twenty on September 6—desperately sought to distinguish himself in combat. He got a new chance on November 25. The day before, Lafayette, his aides, and Brigadier General George Weedon of Virginia rode from Greene's headquarters in Mount Holly to the Continentals' forward base in Haddonfield. The next day, Lafayette reconnoitered and located a vulnerable Hessian picket (outpost) east of Gloucester Town. The local Continental and militia commanders provided Lafayette with a detachment of at least three hundred men, and that afternoon, the marquis attacked and routed the 350-man strong Hessian picket, driving it back almost two and a half miles along King's Road to Gloucester Town. It was a smart little action, but not much more than an annoyance to the British—although with significant consequences for Lafayette and the Revolution.

The following day, November 26, Washington received two reports on the King's Road skirmish: a long letter from Lafayette and a report from Greene. While Greene's report focused on the overall military situation, his half-paragraph description of the King's Road skirmish paid a compliment to Lafayette. It was the first time a senior American officer had noted with approval Lafayette's performance in command. And Washington trusted and listened to Greene. The marquis's letter and Greene's report reached Washington late the same day while Washington was dictating a letter to Henry Laurens, president of the Continental Congress. Washington was working his way through a list of military issues when he received the reports on the skirmish. He immediately switched topics, calling to Laurens's attention his concern that Lafayette might return to France "in disgust" if not afforded an opportunity to assume an active military role. The commander in chief then pointed out that the Continental army had a shortage of major generals, and he recommended that Lafayette be given a division.

Lafayette rejoined the Continental army at Whitemarsh, Pennsylvania, on November 28. There he learned that Congress had agreed with Washington's request that Lafayette be given command of a division, and on December 4, 1777, the marquis took command of the division formerly under Major General Adam Stephen. At Whitemarsh, Lafayette participated in the discussions on where to camp for the winter, and from there he supervised his division as it marched with the rest of the army to Valley Forge.[18] Now a real major general, the marquis became a happy, busy man, responsible for three thousand men, and every fourth or fifth day—as major general of the day—he held the responsibility for the whole Valley Forge encampment. Thus began an increasingly important military and diplomatic career—not to mention Lafayette's rise to iconic status in the pantheon of America's founders. And it all started on King's Road in Gloucester County, New Jersey, November 25, 1777.

THIS BOOK IS ABOUT more than a forty-five-minute battle—actually just a brisk skirmish. And it is about more that the French marquis, central as he is to our story. It also is about the other participants: the Hessian riflemen manning the picket, the detachment of Continental riflemen, and especially, the South Jersey militia. Why were the militia with Lafayette, willing, almost eager, to launch a bayonet charge on the Hessian picket—one of their officers, a twenty-nine-year-old carpenter, calling out "Come well lads" as he jogged out ahead of them? Although seconds later the carpenter suffered a mortal wound, his men charged on. Compared to other militia facing British or German regulars, the performance of these Jerseymen was exemplary. When the enemy challenged Pennsylvania militia, for example, they responded differently. Two weeks later at Whitemarsh, large contingents of Pennsylvania militia panicked and fled on two occasions. What was so different about the South Jersey militia?

Then there were the residents living on the farmlands along the east bank of the Delaware River, a peaceful, even idyllic region before 1777. Most of the skirmish occurred in the Town of Gloucester, Gloucester County's smallest township, and many residents not only heard the guns on November 25, but some of them took cover as the war literally came to their doorsteps. Who were these people, how did they figure in the events of the day, and how did they react to the shock of war?

Finally, all of these matters point to the central theme of this book: small battles are not necessarily of small consequence. Rather, they can influence events in dramatic ways. While historians certainly are aware this is true, studies of the War for Independence have neglected the point when dealing with Lafayette's engagement in November 1777. Theodore Thayer, in his biography of Nathanael Greene, barely mentions that the marquis accompanied Greene to New Jersey. Harlow Giles Unger, in his 2002 biography of Lafayette, allots only a paragraph to the skirmish and two pages to Lafayette's promotion. Mike Duncan, in his new *Hero of Two Worlds* (2021), gives the events of November–December 1777 only one page. The November 2021 biography by Bruce Mowday, *Lafayette at Brandywine: The Making of an American Hero*, does connect the victory on King's Road to Lafayette's promotion, but his description of the action is superficial and contains errors. Earlier biographers provide fuller accounts of the skirmish but fail to fully evaluate its significance. Without this victory, would the Continental Congress have voted to give Lafayette command of a division in the Continental army? No, it would not have done so. Without this promotion, in 1778, the marquis could not have commanded large detachments reconnoitering Philadelphia, May 18–20; at the Battle of Monmouth, June 28; and at the siege of Newport, Rhode Island, in August. Lafayette may well have returned to France in late 1778 a disappointed man. The Revolution would have lost an important lobbyist at the French court, and America would have lost a Revolutionary notable.[19] Thus our volume also fills a gap in the broader history of America's revolutionary struggle and a further understanding of Lafayette's role in it.

Our narrative proceeds in five chapters and a short epilogue. In war, much depends on location, and chapter 1 surveys the terrain and other physical features of the battlefield. It also looks at regional society: Who lived there, and what was life like before war engulfed the region? And what happened when the war came? Chapter 2 moves to the military sphere. The capabilities of Colonel Daniel Morgan's riflemen are well known. Less reported are the capabilities of the South Jersey militia. These were half of the men Lafayette commanded, and we need to know about them. We will trace the militia's transition from a raw and inexperienced organization to a more cohesive force that, by late 1777, could give a good account of itself in combat. Chapter 3 continues the militia story, but in the ominous context of rival British and rebel armies converging on Gloucester County in November—that is, in the run-up to the Battle of Gloucester. Chapter 4 provides a narrative of the engagement itself, Lafayette's "Little Event." Chapter 5 describes the marquis's promotion, his return to France with glowing letters of recommendation from Congress, and the delegates' direction that Lafayette be presented with a golden battle sword. We look at how the skirmish became—through the aegis of none other than Benjamin Franklin—the "Battle of Gloucester," and why. Finally, the epilogue returns to the theme of this introduction. The skirmish on King's Road launched the marquis's brilliant future, a future that ultimately made him a symbol of French support for the American Revolution.

The origins of this book are in *Gloucester, New Jersey: A Forgotten Battle of the American Revolution,* a report to the American Battlefield Protection Program that we completed in July 2019 for the Camden County Historical Society.[20] Our report not only described the skirmish but also described Gloucestertown Township in much more detail than space allows in this book: population, landholdings, and buildings. We registered archaeological sites with the state archaeologist and outlined a series of wayside exhibits for interpreting the skirmish. This report is available from the American Battlefield Protection Program, US Department of the Interior. Other material for this book is drawn from Garry Stone's incomplete draft of a book on the American Revolution in South Jersey.

ONE

The Context of Battle: Land and People

LAFAYETTE'S SKIRMISH, the so-called Battle of Gloucester, fought November 25, 1777, took place almost entirely within Gloucestertown Township, Gloucester County, New Jersey. Like all battles, it did not occur in a vacuum. There was context, the wider war and related operations being obvious examples (to which we will return). But there was also terrain, loosely defined here to include natural and agricultural topography, water courses, roads, and structures of all kinds. Terrain features have always figured prominently in the conduct of military operations and often significantly in the results of those operations. Lafayette, like legions of commanders before and after him, would do his best to learn the "lay of the land" and, as the Duke of Wellington would later put it, to find out what "was at the other side of the hill" before committing to combat.[1] And if terrain mattered, so too did a locale's residents. They often served as sources of intelligence and, in the case of revolutionary New Jersey, as combatant militia. Even if they played no military role, commanders needed to know something of regional loyalties. Whom in the populace could they trust? Who could lead them to supplies and forage? Who knew anything about enemy forces? People counted. So, before we consider the Battle of Gloucester, we need to know more about the land and people of Gloucestertown Township.

THE TOWN OF GLOUCESTER TOWNSHIP

The Battle of Gloucester took place along a 2.4-mile segment of a road known both as Salem and King's Road. At its ends, King's Road connected the towns of Burlington and Salem. Locally, it connected the town of Haddonfield and the courthouse hamlet of Gloucester Town. While the fighting began in western Newton Township,[2] most of the conflict occurred within the Town of Gloucester, the smallest township of eighteenth-century Glouces-ter County. (For convenience, we will refer to the Town of Gloucester as "Gloucestertown Township." Now, the former town-ship includes the Camden County municipalities of Gloucester City, Mt. Ephraim, Brooklawn, Bellmawr, and much of Barrington and Haddon Heights.) Until the British occupied Philadelphia in September 1777, this was prosperous farmland, a patchwork of fields and orchards interspersed with woodland. Yeomen farmer plantations (farms)[3] alternated with the house lots of la-borers and a few artisans.

The township occupied two necks of land formed by creeks draining into the Delaware River. King's Run (or brook) formed most of the northern boundary, while Little Timber Creek split the township into north and south halves. Great Timber Creek and Beaver Branch formed the southern boundary. South of Great Timber Creek was Deptford Township and the thriving town of Woodbury. East of Beaver Branch lay Gloucester Township. The King's Road ran down the center of the northern neck for a mile and three quarters before turning southerly to cross the southern neck and continue to the towns of Woodbury and Salem.

The environs of Gloucester Town were more easily defended than attacked as the creeks limited access. River Road from Cooper's Ferry crossed over a half mile of marsh and water to

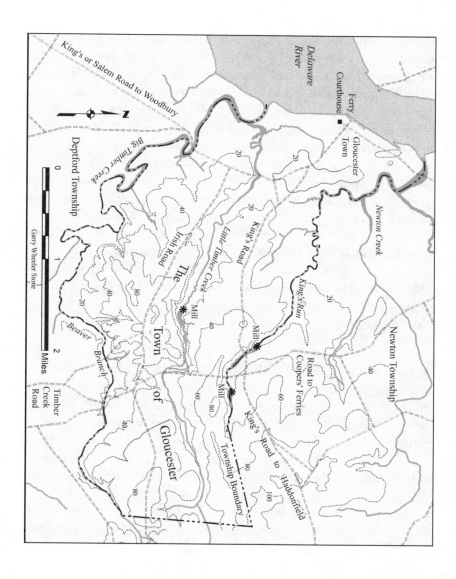

Map 1. The Town of Gloucester: topography, waterways, and roads. Note how creeks and ravines limited access to Gloucester Town. Within this small township there were about 5,493 acres of land, marsh, and water, most of which was owned by 22 property owners.

enter the hamlet. From the south, King's Road first had to cross Great Timber Creek and then, two-thirds of a mile later, cross Little Timber Creek. A road extended from the east, but it joined King's Road south of Little Timber Creek. The only access to Gloucester Town without an easily defended creek crossing was along King's Road from Haddonfield, and even this had limited access. At the eastern township boundary—the King's Run—a wooded hill with mill ponds along part of its eastern side offered a defensive position. Beyond the hill, the road followed the high ground between Little Timber Creek and the King's Run. With ravines and marsh-edged runs narrowing the upland to less than a third of a mile at Archibald's Run, and even less at Mile Run, there was little room for an attacking army to maneuver, while the woods provided cover for a defending army. Conversely, these same woods facilitated *la petite guerre* (guerrilla warfare) by small groups of irregulars. These conditions would shape the events of November 25–27.[4]

GLOUCESTER TOWN

As King's Road turned south toward Woodbury, a branch led west and became High Street of Gloucester Town. The town was the public heart of the county, but in 1777, a stranger riding in might have wondered if he had entered the wrong place. After passing three modest workers' homes at the town's eastern edge, High Street passed through a quarter of a mile of fields, vacant lots, and woodland before—only three hundred yards from the Delaware River—the stranger arrived at the hamlet that was Gloucester Town. It consisted of a courthouse, a large tavern and ferry landing, three other dwellings that sometimes doubled as taverns, a carpenter's dwelling, and—at the northern edge of the hamlet—the sheriff's home. Still farther north stood a second wharf with a storehouse and large dwelling named Lilliput.[5] Beyond Lilliput, Judge Samuel Harrison had his plantation, and at the north end of Gloucester Town, the river road to Cooper's Ferry crossed a large sand hill. A British unit would be posted there November 25–27, 1777.[6] At the toll bridge over Newton Creek, the toll collector and his wife kept a tavern in their home.[7]

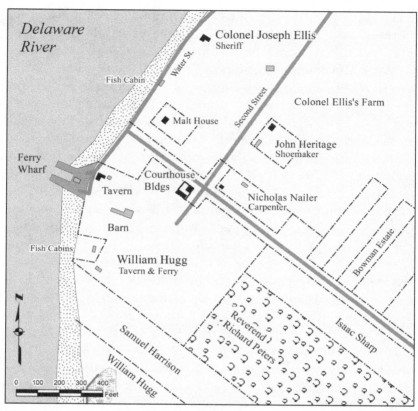

Map 2. Gloucester Town in 1777—only a hamlet. There was one other dwelling near the corner of High and Second Streets, but it cannot be located. Captain Harrison owned the Malt House. British sailors burned it November 26, 1777.

The county courthouse served as the centerpiece for the hamlet, along with an adjacent workhouse. The courthouse comprised a good brick building above a basement jail; the roof featured a shuttered belfry. Gloucester Town was not a large place, but the courthouse impressed some outsiders. In November 1777, a Hessian soldier recorded in his diary that the town was "not very big nor symmetrical, but it does have an imposing townhall."[8]

West of the courthouse, overlooking the ferry landing, stood Hugg's tavern. The tavern provided more than a resting place for travelers. It was a Gloucester County public place almost as important as the courthouse. The county court withdrew to the tavern for dinner, some of the justices lodged there between sessions, and when it was unbearably cold, the court met in the tavern. There auctions were held, county commissioners let contracts, and executors settled estates.[9] In 1774, during the run-up to the Revolution, mass meetings gathered at the courthouse; but the tavern hosted the executive committee of the Gloucester County Committee of Observation (the Whig organization formed to enforce compliance with the boycott of British goods and trade) when it met to organize its May 1775 meeting. And in May, the committee's seventy-seven members met at the tavern to choose delegates to attend the New Jersey Provincial Congress—the congress that began preparations for war with Britain. Of the seven delegates, one became a Loyalist, one retired, and the other five became active rebels: Joseph Ellis and Joseph Hugg of Gloucestertown Township, John Cooper and John Sparks of Deptford Township, and Elijah Clark from the forks of the Mullica River in Galloway Township (map 5, page 25).[10] We will meet these five rebels again.

The tavern also provided the rendezvous for the Gloucester Fox Hunting Club, a group of Philadelphians who rode after the hounds, refreshed themselves in taverns after the hunt, and hosted diner parties for each other. These young gentlemen of means could afford a good horse, hunting attire, and the dues required to maintain a pack of hounds. Equally important, they had the leisure that permitted them to spend days riding through Gloucester County farms and woods. While the original twenty-seven members lived in Philadelphia, two—Tench Francis and Israel Morris—had, or would have, connections to Gloucester County. Moreover, by meeting at Gloucester Town and dining in Gloucester County taverns, they became known to William Hugg's brothers and the local yeomanry. In the mid-1770s, the resulting personal connections facilitated cooperation in defending the port of Philadelphia. Three members of the Pennsylvania Council of Safety were members of the fox-hunting club: Samuel

Morris Jr., Robert Morris, and John Cadwalader. In November 1777, Cadwalader's Gloucester County fox-hunting experience served him well as the Pennsylvania militia general prepared a detailed sketch map of the roads between Billingsport, Haddonfield, and Cooper's Ferry (modern Camden).[11]

Twenty-two members of the Gloucester Fox Hunting Club were the nucleus of the Philadelphia Light Horse, a militia unit established in November 1774. The men possessed good horses, equestrian skills, leisure, and the means to acquire uniforms, sabers, and pistols. Samuel Morris Jr.—field commander of the Light Horse and a manager of the hunt club—would appear at Gloucester Town as a member of the Pennsylvania Council of Safety. Benjamin Randolph was another member of the Philadelphia Light Horse to cross the Delaware. In late 1776, when it seemed the British would capture Philadelphia, Randolph, a Philadelphia cabinetmaker, moved his family to Gloucester County. Several Gloucester County young men would join Randolph and serve with the Philadelphia Light Horse during winter 1777. They formed the beginning of the Gloucester County troop of militia light horse.[12]

POPULATION

Quakers began settling neighboring Newton Township in 1681 and Gloucestertown Township in 1686–1689, so by 1777, the area had hosted three and more generations of settlement.[13] A large proportion of the township's population descended from the original Quaker immigrants, largely English but some Irish, although at least one family descended from a Dutch convert. The cultural landscape included a scattering of other Protestants as well, mostly Anglicans. Indentured servants had arrived from Ireland and the Continent, and some remained after their indentures expired, adding names like McCarty and Peckman to the lists of taxpayers. The largest minority comprised African-American slaves and the descendants of slaves. The census of 1784 reveals that they made up almost 20 percent of the township's population.[14] The September 1777 British occupation of Philadelphia and their occasional incursions into South Jersey provided slaves with escape opportunities. Some did, though apparently not to the extent as in Virginia or even in East New Jersey. One Gloucester Town escapee, however, figures into our story: Dick Ellis, the slave of Gloucester Sheriff and militia Colonel Joseph Ellis. Dick Ellis successfully fled to British protection in Philadelphia, but he would be back to his home territory with royal forces in November—there to confront militia under the command of his former master.[15]

The economy of Gloucestertown Township and adjacent Delaware River townships hinged on their proximity to Philadelphia, the largest city in English America and a busy port with a hungry merchant marine and export markets. City residents and sailors needed meat, poultry, eggs, butter, cheese, vegetables, and fruit. Shipwrights, carpenters, wheelwrights, and a host of other artisans required timber. All needed firewood; smiths needed charcoal. By boat or ferry, farmers and butchers took their produce across the Delaware to the Market or Arch Street landing, and then carried their goods to the Jersey Market, a shed that ran up Market Street from Front Street to Second.[16] Firewood arrived in flatboats carrying up to twelve cords.[17] Most of the township contained good farmland, and Gloucestertown Township landowning planters (farmers) prospered. Most planters ranked in the middling sort—the median farm comprised 235 acres.[18] With population growth, however, the number of smallholders and landless grew.

TOWNSHIP LEADERS

Many of Western Gloucester County's revolutionary or Whig leaders lived in or adjacent to Gloucester Town, such as members of the Harrison and Hugg families, whose third, fourth, and fifth generations enjoyed inherited wealth. Joseph Ellis, the grandson of a Waterford Township settler, joined them in 1759. All were hard-working rebels, but they were more understanding of their Quaker neighbors than were John Cooper and John Sparks of Woodbury, the rivals of the Harrisons and the Huggs for Whig leadership. These local notables—Harrisons, Huggs, and Ellis—are worth knowing; these men led their township and county into revolution and war.

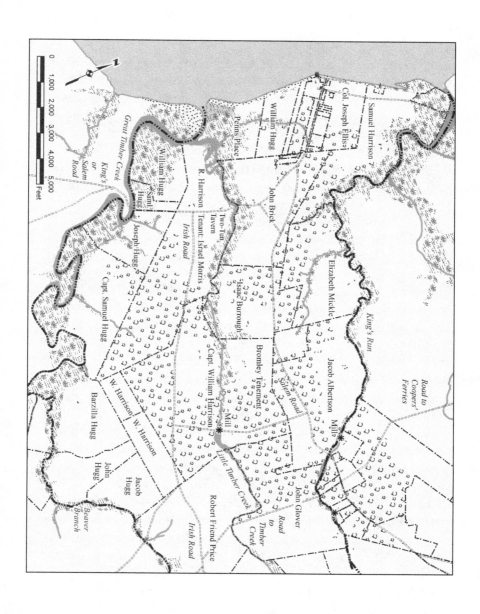

Map 3. Town of Gloucester: principal landowners in 1777.

The Harrisons

Judge Samuel Harrison III lived in a big brick house overlooking the Delaware River and the lush meadows at the mouth of Newton Creek. A grandparent had constructed the house there. Samuel II built a brick addition, and in 1756, Samuel III replaced the original portion of the house with a two-story brick structure (gallery, fig. 15).

From his father and grandfather, Samuel Harrison III inherited land, social status, and ambition. His grandfather, Samuel Harrison, a mariner, arrived at Gloucester Town in the mid-1680s.[19] His sons became prominent Gloucester County yeomen farmers. The oldest son, William, served as sheriff, justice of the peace, and a member of the assembly. His brother, Samuel II, served four three-year terms as sheriff before being appointed a judge in the county court. He died in early 1762, and the following June, Samuel Harrison III took his father's seat as a judge on the county court.[20] As the justice living closest to the courthouse, he played an important role in legal proceedings between quarterly court sessions.[21] His role increased after the British closure of the port of Boston roiled New Jersey political life.

New Jersey protests began in June 1774, and on July 18, the county's "respectable inhabitants" met at the courthouse, where they chose Harrison to serve on a Committee of Correspondence. In December, to enforce the October 24 resolves of the Continental Congress, the committee expanded and became the Committee of Observation with Judge Samuel Harrison named as chairman. The committee sent delegates to New Jersey provincial conventions and congresses, collected funds for the relief of the poor in Boston, enforced the resolves of the Continental Congress, and, beginning in mid-1775, began preparations to defend New Jersey against British invasion. In July, Harrison, his nephew Joseph Hugg (clerk of the committee), and others met with the Philadelphia Committee of Safety to plan the installation of chevaux de Frise in the Delaware River. During fall 1775 and January 1776, Harrison placed orders with fellow justice Richard Somers, merchant of Great Egg Harbor, for £150 of gunpowder for distribution to the township militia companies.[22]

Busy as a judge and chairman of the Committee of Observation, Harrison did not attend the statewide meetings that prepared for war and wrote a new constitution. When the new state government appointed county judges and justices in September 1776, Samuel Harrison III was not reappointed. Thus, the court lost the voice of a moderate Whig.[23]

Judge Harrison's cousin, William Harrison Jr., was captain of the Gloucestertown Township militia company—one of the units of Colonel Joseph Ellis's 2nd Gloucester Regiment. Harrison lived on the south side of Little Timber Creek two miles southeast of the courthouse (gallery, fig. 16). There he had inherited over six hundred acres from his father, William Harrison Sr. Only documentary fragments have survived of the son's militia service, but he probably received a first lieutenant's commission when the county revived its militias in 1775, then was elevated to captain when Ellis became colonel, and served throughout the war. He was in the field in November 1777 and with Ellis at Somerset Courthouse in January 1777. From May 1777 to July 19, 1778, he was major, and then major commandant, of Forman's Additional Continental Regiment. As a Continental officer, he fought in the Battle of Germantown, October 4, 1777; with Lafayette, November 25, 1777; and—attached to the 2nd New Jersey Regiment—in South Jersey, April to June 1778. Back in the Gloucester militia, he served along the Raritan, and at South Amboy. In the nineteenth century, aged survivors of the company remembered Harrison as "an active and efficient officer" who enjoyed his status and its symbols: cocked hat, blue coat, and sword.[24]

The Huggs

More numerous than the Harrisons, the Huggs descended from immigrant John Hugg, who in 1685 purchased almost one thousand acres between Great and Little Timber Creeks. In the 1770s, the family owned six tracts along the north bank of Great Timber Creek, a series of plantations that stretched from the Delaware to just east of Beaver Branch. The three sons of William Hugg, innkeeper, owned the three western plantations. When William died in 1775, he bequeathed a plantation and the Gloucester

Town tavern to his youngest son, William Jr.[25] Perhaps as befitting a host, William Jr. did not actively engage in politics, while his brothers, Joseph and Samuel, were conspicuous rebels. Although Joseph and Samuel Hugg would not gain title to their Great Timber Creek plantations until their father died, they had been farming there since about the time of their marriages. In 1773–1774, Samuel paid taxes on 115 acres, 21 head of horses and cattle, and 3 adult male slaves, while Joseph remitted payment for 186 acres and 30 head of horses and cattle. Only Judge Harrison had a larger herd than Joseph Hugg.[26]

Joseph Hugg was one of the most active Whigs of Gloucester County. Before the Revolution, he had demonstrated his competence while serving as clerk for the freeholders[27] and as sheriff. In 1774, the Committee of Correspondence and its successor, the Committee of Observation, chose Joseph Hugg as clerk, and in September 1776, the justices of the county court elected him their clerk. By December 1776, Joseph Hugg was a commissary (purchasing agent) for the Continental army. In partnership with his neighbor Israel Morris, Hugg purchased pork, beef, salt, and spirits for the army. During the Whitemarsh and Valley Forge encampments, Hugg and South Jersey became an important source of supplies. In November 1777, an army commissary described salt from Hugg as "the finest you ever saw."[28]

By the 1770s, Joseph Hugg was a well-established planter farming his father's Great Timber Creek plantation (William Hugg Sr. had moved to the Gloucester Town tavern in 1746). He prospered and added a modest, two-story brick addition to his father's old frame house (gallery, fig. 17). With his fees as sheriff augmenting his agricultural income, in 1771, he acquired the famous racehorse Yorick and advertised Yorick's stud fee as "TWENTY SHILLINGS the single leap, FORTY SHILLINGS the season."[29]

In February 1776, the Provincial Congress resolved to raise two artillery companies to serve for one year as "State Troops" (state troops served continuously for the time stated in the establishing legislation, whereas militia served alternate months, if needed). Samuel Hugg volunteered to raise one of the companies. He lived with his wife, Mary, on the next plantation east of his brother Joseph in a small but fine brick farmhouse (gallery fig. 18).[30] Like other Huggs, Samuel possessed wealth. He probably had an easy time getting the commission: neighbor Colonel Joseph Ellis served as a member of the Provincial Congress's military committees. However, it proved difficult to recruit the men (matrosses) needed to work the company's two field pieces. Hugg and his two lieutenants had to scour Gloucester, Salem, and Cumberland Counties to find men willing to leave home for a year. They did find forty-seven men, trained in Salem County, and in July marched north to New Brunswick. With Washington's army, they retreated into Pennsylvania, crossed back, and fought at Trenton, Assunpink Creek, and Princeton. One of Hugg's privates died at Princeton in April 1777: Levi Albertson of Gloucestertown Township. At the end of their twelve months, Captain Hugg and some of his men went home, Hugg discharging them at his house on Great Timber Creek. Others stayed and became the nucleus of a Continental army artillery company.[31]

While Captain Hugg's state service had ended, he remained on the county militia rolls. So Hugg joined "gentlemen of character" who had formed a light horse troop attached to Ellis's 2nd Gloucester Regiment. Then Ellis secured two brass 6-pounders and asked Hugg to organize a county artillery company. Franklin Davenport, a rising young lawyer of Gloucestertown Township, joined as captain lieutenant, and Benjamin Whitall, a yeoman farmer of Woodbury, joined as lieutenant. As if farming and light horse, and artillery service did not engage them enough, Samuel Hugg and Franklin Davenport assisted Joseph Hugg and Israel Morris in gathering supplies for the Continental army.[32]

Joseph Ellis

Joseph Ellis (c.1730–1796) was South Jersey's outstanding soldier. He was born in Waterford Township where his Quaker parents prospered as farmers. In 1758, when New Jersey raised a new regiment to fight in the French and Indian War (the Seven Years' War), Joseph Ellis volunteered, received an appointment as captain, marched north, and took part in the unsuccessful attack on

Fort Ticonderoga. For this, the local Religious Society of Friends (Quakers) read him out of meeting (excommunicated him).

In 1759, Ellis arrived in Gloucester Town as a journeyman tanner. He was nothing if not enterprising. He purchased town lots and ten acres of meadow from Samuel Harrison, built a tanyard, and on the first day of January 1760, he married Mary Hinchman. A year later, Abigail Ellis was born. By 1764, probably a widower, Captain Ellis apparently grew tired of tanning. In April, as he prepared to enlist a second time in the New Jersey Regiment, he advertised to lease for seven years his tanyard, his three slave tanners, and his home: "a very good House, and a small Plantation." His advertisement failed to attract a tenant, but nevertheless, he led another company of men north to the New York frontier. Upon his return, Ellis resumed tanning.[33]

Ellis returned from New York with enhanced prestige. His tanyard and small (65-acre) plantation provided modest prosperity, and his place of residence adjacent to the courthouse kept him visible. His home was an ancient structure, the front section built at the end of the seventeenth century. The one-and-a-half-story house, unpretentious and roomy, proved to be a convenient location for Ellis as he became active in Gloucester County politics (gallery, fig. 14).[34]

And he was very active. On July 18, 1774, in a meeting at the courthouse, he won election as a member of the county's Committee of Correspondence; the committee members then elected him treasurer, and later, a delegate to the Whig Provincial Congress. Captain Ellis was slow to arrive at the Congress—having been appointed high sheriff of Gloucester County in May 1775—but as soon as he arrived, the delegates appointed him to sit on all military committees. By October he had received a commission as colonel of Gloucester's 2nd Regiment. As sheriff, Ellis could not join the state troops helping defend New York Harbor in late 1776, but as soon as the British invaded New Jersey and Governor William Livingston called out the militia, Ellis entered the field. He led the 2nd Gloucester County Regiment men in the skirmishing at Mount Holly in December 1776, and the following January found Colonel Ellis at Somerset Court House (modern Millstone) in central New Jersey drilling men from Gloucester County.[35]

Among Whig leaders, Joseph Ellis was unusual. He was both an early advocate of complete independence and a humane man (albeit a slave owner) who understood that honorable men could disagree. Many, if not most, rebels were wont to treat Loyalists harshly; and many saw Quakers as tainted with loyalism because of the Friends' pacifism and desire to remain out of the political controversies of the day. Quakers faced fines and public insult for their principled refusals to pledge allegiance to the new revolutionary authorities, pay the imposed military tax, or turn out for militia duty. But Ellis, perhaps reflecting his Quaker roots, took a more moderate stance. On January 20, 1777, three Deptford magistrates arrested two prominent Quaker leaders for refusing to swear allegiance to New Jersey's rebel government. Sheriff Ellis befriended the men, housed them in his own home until their cell could be cleaned, frequently visited them, and facilitated their release. Ellis's combination of martial and administrative aptitude, political skill, and humanity helped the 2nd Militia District avoid the turmoil that would roil other parts of the county as Whigs, Loyalists, and neutrals confronted one another.[36]

Of course, other local families and individuals played roles in Gloucester's affairs, including the area's contributions to the revolutionary effort—and we will meet some of them soon enough. But the prominence of Ellis and the extended Hugg and Harrison families did illustrate a key point: a congruence existed between social and economic influence and military leadership. Society's "betters" made up the majority of Gloucester's senior militia officers—a matter to which we will return.

THE BATTLEFIELD PLANTATIONS

On November 25, 1777, plundering, enemy occupation, and skirmishing threatened the lives and possessions of the prosperous and the poor alike who lived along the two-and-a-half-mile portion of King's Road constituting the battlefield. From the 1779 tax list that Assessor Jacob Albertson compiled, we know their names, economic status, and, in many cases, their occupations. It was a diverse group, illustrating the complexity of rural life. Yeoman farmers and their servants occupied four of the eight substantial plantations, the widow of a former sheriff occupied another, a well-equipped sharecropper worked one, and one provided housing for a laborer and his family, as did a subsidiary plantation. Because of the war, a ninety-three-acre plantation stood vacant. The tax roll also included two smallholders, three mills with their associated structures, and a weaver's house lot.[37]

Lafayette's fight, as we will see, began near the western boundary of Newton Township near the intersection of King's Road and the road from Timber Creek to the Coopers' ferries. Benjamin and Mary Bates lived on an eighteen-acre lot at the northwest corner—not enough land for agriculture to have supported the family. Benjamin Bates may have been a logger and sawyer living part time in Newton Township. He owned a 200-acre plantation, 1,300 acres of woodland, and a quarter-share of a sawmill in Gloucester Township.[38] Near the southeastern corner on a four-acre lot lived Samuel and Mary Brown in a house bustling with children. A weaver, Brown also operated a fulling mill for his neighbor, John Glover. Fullers washed and stretched woven woolen cloth, dyeing it if requested, and cleaned clothes. A member of the Religious Society of Friends, Brown, "for refusing to Train or Bear Arms," had property seized in lieu of the fines the rebel Provincial Congress imposed. (However, the value of the seized property equaled less than half of the legislated fines.)[39]

King's Run—the eastern boundary of Gloucestertown Township—provided power for two mills. John Glover owned the upper mill. The water from the fulling mill tailrace fed the pond for Jacob Albertson's gristmill complex—King's Road crossed the King's Run on Albertson's milldam. Albertson probably used coarse particles screened from flour and meal to feed his hogs, for in 1779, he was the township's foremost pork producer. Jacob and Mary Albertson lived west of the run on the northern part of a 238-acre plantation. The Albertsons owned a small plantation south of the road. It appears Dennis McCarty, householder,[40] occupied it as

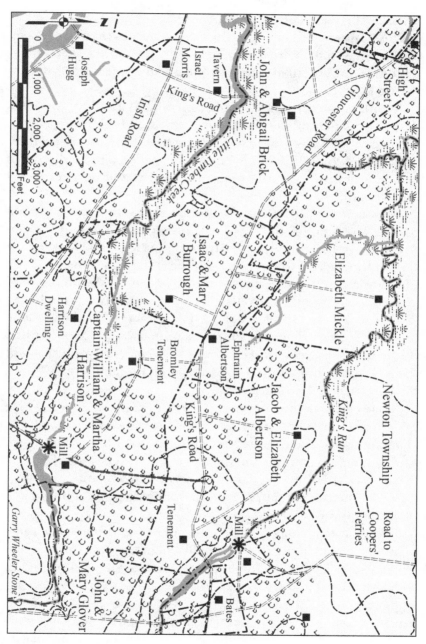

Map 4. Battlefield Plantations in 1777.

a likely Albertson employee. McCarty was on the township militia roster.[41] Albertson, serving as township constable as well as tax assessor, may have gained exemption from militia service.[42] A cousin, Ephraim Albertson, lived on an adjacent thirty-four-acre house lot.

South of the Albertsons' land, John and Mary Glover owned a 262-acre plantation. John worked as a weaver, fuller, and yeoman planter. Both Glovers were devout Quakers; John was an overseer in the Haddonfield Friends business meeting. Their adherence to the Friends' principles of nonviolence would be a recurring problem for their military-age sons.[43]

Between the Glovers' lands and the Delaware River, five plantations and a mill abutted Little Timber Creek. Captain William Harrison Jr. had inherited two from his father.[44] The first tract, a seventy-one-acre parcel, contained the stone and frame gristmill that the captain's father constructed. The lane to the mill crossed the dam and provided a convenient short cut between the King's and Irish Roads. On October 22, 1777, a large Hessian detachment—forced to detour because of a dismantled bridge—crossed Little Timber Creek on Harrison's milldam.[45] Beyond the mill lane Harrison owned the 156-acre Bromley tenant farm. Charles Saxton farmed it on shares.

Isaac and Mary Burrough owned the next property, a 190-acre plantation. It included twenty-seven acres of meadow along Little Timber Creek, their house, outbuildings, a "commodious barn, with suitable partitions for the stock, and a threshing floor," a small orchard, and one hundred acres of woodland. Excellent farmers, the Burroughs paid off the purchase price of their plantation in just four years.[46]

The plantations along this section of King's Road had a median size of 220 acres, slightly smaller than the township median of 235 acres and comparable to the median size of Burlington County's Chester Township plantations.[47] They survived the forages of 1777–1778 surprisingly well. The numbers of horses and cattle present on these plantations represent a 20 percent reduction from the 1773 count, but *only* 20 percent. Either these farm-

NAME	OCCUPATION OR STATUS OTHER THAN YEOMAN FARMER	ACRES	HOUSE HOLDER	SINGLE MEN WITH HORSE	SLAVES	LIVESTOCK		
						HORSES	CATTLE	HOGS
Albertson, Jacob	Gristmill, assessor	238			1	5	4	34
McCarty, Dennis	Employee, Albertson?		X					
Saxton, Charles	Tenant, W. Harrison	156	X			4	8	18
Saxton, Daniel	Employee, C. Saxton?		X					
Harrison, Capt. Wm.	Gristmill	71						
Mickle, Elizabeth	Widow	225					1	
Morris, Israel				1	1		1	
Davenport, Franklin	Attorney, Surrogate				1	2		
Burrough, Isaac, Jr.		160			1	4	9	10
Albertson, Joseph	*Employee, John Brick	147	X			1	1	
Brick, John	*	73				6	9	15
Penn's Place	Vacant	93						
Spire, John	Employee, S. Harrison?		X			2	2	
Harrison, Samuel	Assessor, former Judge	235			2	3	11	1

*Farmed as one 220-acre plantation. Source: New Jersey State Archives, Ratable book 720.

Table 1. Residents from the King's Run to the Town of Gloucester Town, 1779.

ers had been diligent in concealing their stock in the woods or they had the savings needed to replenish their herds. Rapid swine reproduction might explain why the large number of hogs features so prominently in the 1779 ratable (tax) list. The number of horses and cattle quickly rebounded to 1773 levels. By 1782, the number of hogs in the township had declined by 22 percent.[48]

Ratable lists—the tax rolls listing lands, livestock, mills, and other taxed property—provide invaluable information for studying the social structure of the era, but only in a gross way. We rely on planters' diaries, newspaper real estate advertisements, probate inventories, and similar documents to learn the details of the local agricultural economy. A probate inventory survives for this section of King's Road: the 1780 inventory of John Brick.

Beyond the Burroughs' land stood the two plantations of John and Abigail Brick. The Bricks came to Gloucestertown Township in June 1766 and, like the Burroughs, thrived as yeoman farmers—adding a brick addition to their log home. Then John died in early 1780. On April 11, court-appointed appraisers inventoried his movable and personal property. Their carefully compiled list documents the complexities of eighteenth-century agriculture and the life of a yeoman family.

Despite having had enemy troops encamped on their property in November 1777, in 1779, the Bricks' farm was reasonably well stocked. They owned five horses and two colts, a yoke of oxen, seven cows, a heifer and four yearlings, sixteen sheep, hogs, poultry, and two beehives. In the barn and in the dwelling loft, the appraisers found fodder (hay and cornstalks), corn, rye, and buckwheat, and the fall-planted winter wheat and rye were growing in the Bricks' fields. In the barn and dwelling, the appraisers listed evidence of dairying and other household manufactures: a cheese press, a cider press, two stills, farm-made wine, and flax. John Brick sold regularly at the Jersey Market in Philadelphia. John and Abigail Brick had seven children, and the household included an African American indentured servant who had two more years to serve. A married employee, Joseph Albertson, householder, lived on their eastern plantation. [49]

One more plantation existed before reaching the Delaware River: Penn's Place, a ninety-three-acre farm and fishery. It had a brick dwelling, orchard, extensive banked hay meadows, and valuable fishing rights.[50] The dwelling apparently had no lessee—a victim of the economic collapse resulting from the September 1777 embargo of British-occupied Philadelphia. The same was true of two-acre Lilliput with its wharf, storehouse, dwelling, and barn. Gloucester felt the economic impact of the war well before Cornwallis came to town.

North of King's Road, only one tract stood between Jacob Albertson's land and the two Gloucester Town farms of Judge Samuel Harrison: the 225-acre Mickle Grove plantation of widow Elizabeth Mickle. Her husband, former sheriff John Mickle, had died in late spring 1774. In 1773, with the help of two male slaves, John Mickle's farming operation had been one of the township's largest, but his widow freed their slaves and liquidated most of the movable estate, retaining only one milk cow. Mickle Grove was down a long lane from King's Road, and the distance from the main thoroughfare may have saved it from plundering in November 1777.[51] In 1779, Elizabeth Mickle had two boarders: attorney and militia officer Franklin Davenport and Israel Morris, assistant continental commissary, a refugee. Enemy soldiers had burned his farm on November 24, 1777.

This, then, made up the battlefield: a busy road flanked by houses, fields, and woodlots. Until the British marched into Philadelphia, its economy thrived. All the owners of good-sized plantations had advanced into the ranks of the yeomanry—the prosperous land-owning farmers able to employ servants and farm on a commercial scale. With land becoming scarcer and more expensive, it remained uncertain whether the young men just starting out—Dennis McCarty, Joseph Albertson, and others—would be as successful. Whatever their status, residents of the battlefield plantations would see their lives and livelihoods impacted, however briefly, by the coming clash of arms.

TWO

War

WHEN THE REVOLUTIONARY CAUSE transitioned from political opposition to actual rebellion—that is, armed resistance—New Jersey's initial military effort centered on the state militia. The New Jersey Provincial Congress passed the first militia act in June 1775, and the new state legislature repeatedly revised it over the next five years. New Jersey's militia—its part-time citizen soldiers—became the core of the state's contribution to the revolutionary struggle. While the state contributed four battalions and part of a fifth to the Continental army, the Continental Congress repeatedly asked for more men, and the state government sought and later drafted volunteers from within the militia.[1] The governor was, and still is, commander in chief of New Jersey's armed forces. From 1776 to 1790, William Livingston filled this role. A prolific Whig propagandist, former delegate to the Continental Congress (1774–1776), and militia brigadier general (1775–1776), and a competent, hard-working rebel leader, Livingston accomplished all these tasks with great aplomb as he became one of the longest-serving and most-effective war governors.[2]

In its early encounters with European professional soldiers, however, the militia did not cover itself with glory. It was not a matter of courage: plenty of militiamen were brave enough, but being largely inexperienced, they faltered time and again. In late 1776, a Loyalist spy reported that one assemblage of southern New Jersey militia consisted of "near one half boys."[3] They often entered the field indifferently equipped and frequently led by officers with little (and sometimes no) command experience. During Washington's retreat across New Jersey, the militia all too often failed the test of combat, dispersing in front of the British invasion. Indeed, Washington had some particularly bitter words for the Jerseymen.[4] Yet in late 1777, the South Jersey militia served Lafayette well. The local troops effectively cooperated with Continental regulars and proved effective combatants under competent local officers. What had happened over the course of a year? How had the militia, including the Gloucester militia, transformed from ill-disciplined amateurs into troops able to carry the fight to the enemy? The story of that transition—our concern in this chapter—is critical in understanding the Battle of Gloucester.

THE GLOUCESTER COUNTY MILITIA

Gloucester County militiamen formed three regiments. The 1st Regiment recruiting area encompassed the Delaware River townships below Great Timber Creek, the 2nd Regimental district covered the Delaware River townships between Great Timber Creek and Burlington County, and the 3rd Regimental district comprised the Atlantic coast townships of Egg Harbor and Galloway.

Leadership lay with men of local social and economic status. In November 1777, the colonels of the three regiments were a physician, a merchant, and the sheriff of the county—all prominent men. The 2nd and 3rd Regiments served under the same colonels for the duration of the Revolution. The 1st Regiment was not as fortunate. Its first colonel, Israel Shreve, a yeoman farmer of 330 acres in Deptford Township, also was a justice of the peace. However, on November 28, 1776, Shreve became a colonel in the Continental army. The regiment's major, Robert Taylor, replaced Shreve, but on September 16, 1777, Taylor submitted his resignation, "on Account of some Dissatisfaction amongst the Officers and Privates of said Battalion," and the legislature commissioned Bodo Otto, Esq., to replace Taylor.[5]

Colonel Bodo Otto (1748–1782), a well-respected physician, justice of the peace, and Episcopal vestryman, took command over the 1st Regiment at a difficult time. Ten days later, the British marched into Philadelphia and the Continental army and state of New Jersey blockaded Philadelphia, crushing South Jersey's economy. The cultural diversity of his district added to Otto's problems, as did the abrasive intolerance some district Whig leaders harbored toward local Quakers and anyone suspected of loyalty to or even sympathy with the Crown. Justices John Cooper, John Sparks, and Thomas Denny jailed men who refused to support the Whig rebellion, and Otto's militiamen became more and more aggressive in collecting fines for not mustering and pressing horses and wagons for use by the militia and army. Loyalists, neutrals, and even former Whigs grew angrier and angrier. Otto's regiment held together during the rest of 1777, but in March 1778, the 1st Regiment disintegrated during a Loyalist uprising.[6]

Unlike Colonel Otto, Richard Somers (1737–1793), colonel of Gloucester's 3rd Regiment, never had to question the loyalty of the men of his district. If the war brought economic woes to the Delaware River townships, the conflict provided a boost to the economy along the Atlantic coast. Like Somers, an investor in many private warships, many of his men benefited from privateering.[7] A merchant, Somers was a Great Egg Harbor justice of the peace, a former delegate to the Provincial Congress, and a member of the township's foremost family. As a merchant trading with the West Indies, Colonel Somers had a leading role in supplying the Gloucester County militia with powder, lead, and gunflints. He appears to have been a competent commander.[8] The other senior 3rd Regiment officers were also men of means. Merchant and Lieutenant Colonel Elijah Clark also owned a mill complex. The regiment's major, Richard Westcott, owned a well-stocked plantation, a woodland, a sawmill, and shares in another sawmill and an ironworks.[9]

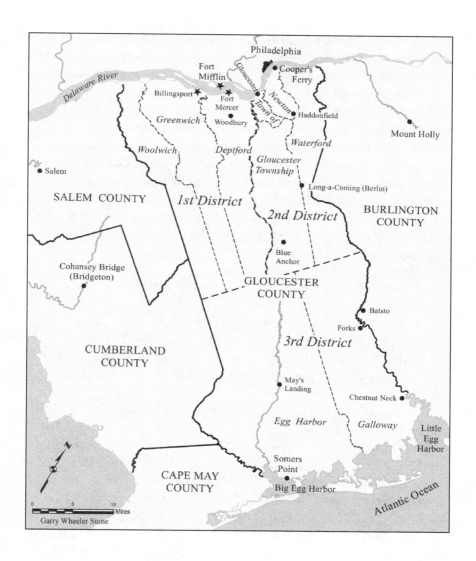

Map 5. Gloucester County Townships and Militia Districts during the American Revolution. At an unknown date, Deptford Township was added to the 2nd District.

We've already met Joseph Ellis, colonel of the 2nd Regiment. He was one of Gloucester's leading men and one of New Jersey's leading soldiers. The 2nd Regiment's other leaders were prosperous yeomen. In Gloucester Township, Lieutenant Colonel Josiah Hillman farmed 294 acres and owned a gristmill; Major William Ellis, the colonel's cousin, farmed 180 acres in nearby Waterford Township.[10] Like their battalion leaders, Delaware River township company commanders also owned property. William Harrison, captain of the Gloucestertown Township company, held the largest amount of land in the township (592 acres, gristmill, and a vessel). In Deptford Township, Captain Jehu Woods farmed 189 acres, while in lower Waterford Township, Captain Jacob Browning farmed 258 acres and managed a fishery. In Newton Township, young Captain John Stokes was only a householder, but his house stood on his father's four-hundred-acre farm, which he would inherit.[11] Subordinate company officers—lieutenants and ensigns—tended to be younger and lower in social status than captains, majors, and colonels. Captain John Stokes's lieutenants consisted of Haddonfield clerks or mechanics. Cumberland County Lieutenant David Mulford, mortally wounded November 25, was a twenty-nine-year-old carpenter.[12]

The economies of Great Egg Harbor and Galloways Townships differed greatly from those of the Delaware River townships. While settlement along the coast began in the late seventeenth century, near-frontier conditions prevailed in large portions of these sprawling townships. Hunting and trapping provided important income, and, because of the poorer soils, agriculture was less important. In Great Egg Harbor, the median farm comprised only one hundred acres.[13] In Galloway Township, a larger gulf existed between the wealthy and the commonality; the median plantation comprised only thirty acres.[14] Hence, the Atlantic township company officers consisted of men with less wealth than their Delaware River peers. In late 1777, tavern keeper George Payne, owner (1781) of a one-hundred-acre plantation and an unimproved seventy-five-acre tract, captained the 3rd Regiment's 1st Company (Galloway Township). His first lieutenant owned 10 acres, his second lieutenant owned 25 acres and 140 acres of woods, while his ensign owned a 50-acre farm. Some officers owned less. John Estell, captain of the 4th Company (Galloway), and his ensign were only householders. Third Regiment company officer candidates were elected by their men based more on personal qualities rather than economic standing.[15]

Throughout the Gloucester County regiments, the social and economic gap between commissioned officers and enlisted men could be—but was not always—substantial. A partial payroll from September 1777 for Captain Samuel Hugg's 2nd Regiment artillery company illustrates the point. Of the six matrosses (privates), three were illiterate or semiliterate—they signed with their marks. Captain Hugg, of the extended and influential Hugg family, lived in a fine brick dwelling. His captain lieutenant, Franklin Davenport, whom we have already met, was a rising lawyer and clerk of Burlington County, while Lieutenant Benjamin Whitall was a yeoman farmer.[16] Whitall deserves special attention. He was the son of Quaker parents of considerable wealth, and his mother's obsessive asceticism drove him from the faith. He first encountered trouble for helping organize a horse race. Then in 1770–71, he and his wife refused to apologize adequately for "unchaste Freedom" before marriage, and the Woodbury Meeting excommunicated the couple.[17]

THE MILITIA GAIN EXPERIENCE

By late 1777, many of the militiamen had gained experience as soldiers. The first major mobilization of New Jersey militia came in June 1776, as a British invasion approached New York. New Jersey answered the call from the Continental Congress for 3,300 militia to serve until December 1. From South Jersey, Colonel Silas Newcomb of Cumberland County led a battalion of young men to New York. Two companies joined from western Gloucester County—Benjamin Whitall led one—but their service proved inglorious. Command shunted them to the reserves at the Battle of Long Island, after which they retreated, dug fortifications, retreated, and retreated. In late November, after accompanying Washington to New Brunswick, they went home. Their service time over, their ranks were thinned by disease, their clothing was worn out, and some men returned home shoeless.[18] Their training, however, would prove quite useful.

And the experience deepened. In late December, Gloucester County militia became part of a South Jersey battalion and participated in operations in the Mount Holly area and later saw service at Second Trenton (Assunpink Creek) on January 2, 1777, and at the Battle of Princeton on January 3.[19] Colonel Ellis, however, stayed behind when the battalion marched north the second time. From Haddonfield, Ellis issued orders mustering two more companies: Captain William Harrison's Gloucestertown Township company and Captain Charles Fisher's Deptford Township company. At the beginning of January, the two companies, Ellis, and his major and cousin, William Ellis, crossed to Philadelphia. There they completed arming from Continental stores and joined Lieutenant Colonel Josiah Hillman and other South Jersey men. Ellis then led them on a three-day march to the village of Somerset Court House on the Millstone River. At Somerset Court House, Harrison's men quartered in three farmhouses and marched into the village every day to drill under Ellis.[20] Then Ellis returned to Gloucester County to resume his duties as sheriff, leaving Hillman in charge of the Gloucester County men. They rotated home, but other South Jersey men replaced them and joined Central Jersey men in routing enemy foragers at Van Neste's mill (January 20).[21] Into early summer, other rotations of South Jersey men joined Continental army detachments in skirmishing with British and German troops along the Raritan River.[22] It had been a difficult twelve months, but South Jersey militia had learned that if they attacked with spirit and with numbers they could defeat regulars—or at least give a good account of themselves. They were becoming veterans; the following months would reinforce this lesson.

In fact, some militiamen became long-term soldiers. For young, laboring-class men, militia service provided an acceptable part- or full-time job. A variety of motivations can be conjectured—a desire to see more of the world, a thirst for adventure, escape from an unhappy home, the monotony of agricultural or woodland labor, or the income from steady militia service. At least sixteen veterans of Gloucester County's 3rd Regiment filed for federal pensions. Eight of these men volunteered for considerable extra time under arms, apparently as paid substitutes for militiamen who hired them rather than serve personally in the ranks—a practice allowed under state laws. Opportunities to serve afloat also existed. New Jersey's many rivers and coastal inlets hosted countless privateers who served for profit under state-issued letters of marque. While time on a privateer could not be claimed as military service, at least four of these pension applicants also had served on privateers.[23] Whether in ranks as substitutes or serving normal rotations of duty, by late 1777, the militia had seen and learned a great deal of war.

DEFENDING THE DELAWARE

For the militia of South Jersey, service in North Jersey provided a diversion from the protection of their homes and livelihoods. The extensive coast lines of Gloucester, Cape May, Cumberland, and Salem Counties made them vulnerable to naval attack. If New Jersey's extensive coastline made it vulnerable, however, it also made it difficult to blockade, and rebel privateering flourished. Beginning in late 1775 and continuing through 1782, shoreline firefights occurred on a fairly regular basis between the crews of British vessels and county militias. When the locals could mobilize quickly, they had considerable success in driving off British naval parties on the Atlantic and Delaware flanks of southern New Jersey. Driving off seaborne raids, however, solved only part of the problem. Soon enough, the men of Gloucester and the other Delaware River counties found plenty to do on their own turf of considerably greater importance.

No concern proved more significant than the defense of the Delaware River approaches to Philadelphia. The city was the economic powerhouse of the mid-Atlantic and the meeting place of the insurgent Continental Congress. And because western Gloucester County was, in effect, a suburb of Philadelphia, Gloucester militia figured in rebel plans to hold the vital port and the river for the revolutionary cause. Preparations to defend river approaches to the city began in earnest some three months after Lexington and Concord. In July 1775, the Pennsylvania Committee of Safety appointed a subcommittee for the "Construction of Boats and Machines" and solicited proposals to construct a flotilla of "galleys"—fifty-foot, shallow-draft gunboats. Before the end of September, thirteen had been launched, each armed with a heavy gun mounted in the bow. These galleys could be rowed or sailed. With completion of the galleys, the Committee of Safety contracted for the construction of smaller guard boats, floating batteries, and fire rafts. By January 1776, the building program was well underway.[24]

Yet no one expected these small craft to confront the Royal Navy alone; they would not have stood a chance against British men-of-war. Committee members also planned to impede naval attack by narrowing the river channel with "machines"—leaving only a narrow gap that could be closed with a chain. Francophile Benjamin Franklin appears to have renamed these machines chevaux-de-Frise—Frisian horses—after an imagined likeness to northern European defenses against cavalry. They consisted of thirty-foot square, open-topped timber boxes armed with two or three giant, iron-tipped pikes. The galley crews floated the boxes to the desired location and sank them with stone ballast. There they rested on the bottom of the river with their spears pointing downstream—the spear tips just below the surface of the river.[25] They proved highly effective obstructions to river navigation, much to the frustration of British sailors.

On July 4, 1775, Committee of Safety members resolved to cross the river to Red Bank, Gloucester County, "to take a view of the River and Islands." They did not venture into the unknown. Committeemen Samuel Morris, John Cadwalader, and Robert Morris, all active members of the Gloucester Fox Hunting Club headquartered at Hugg's Tavern, knew the landscape well. After investigating the ship channel, they returned on July 16 to inquire if Gloucester County would assist in defending the Delaware River. Two days later, the Gloucester committee furnished a list of fourteen landowners willing to donate a total of 296 logs—Benjamin Whitall promised fifty-five.[26] The ship channel ran close to Billingsport and between Fort Island and Red Bank, and Gloucester County timber could be easily floated or dragged to the shore. Over the next twenty-one months, contractors constructed at least sixty-seven frames for chevaux-de-Frise at Gloucester County landings, each requiring twenty-five to thirty logs and hundreds of board feet of two-inch plank.[27] The committee's decision to obstruct the Delaware with chevaux-de-Frise created additional employment for Gloucester County woodland laborers and sawmill operators.

In February 1776, the Committee of Safety turned its attention to protecting the chevaux-de-Frise. Could New Jersey artillery batteries keep the British navy from grappling and pulling apart the obstructions? The Continental Congress offered to pay for the work, and on July 2, 1776, Congress took title to one hundred acres at Billingsport, overlooking the Delaware where the ship channel ran close to the Jersey shore. The Pennsylvania Committee of Safety hired a French engineer to lay out a fort, and well-known Philadelphia architect and revolutionary Robert Smith (who had designed the chevaux-de-Frise) began construction of barracks.[28] The work lagged, however, as the fort construction competed with the building of chevaux-de-Frise, naval vessels, and privateers. Further delays resulted from the death of Smith in February 1777. Colonel John Bull, a Pennsylvania infantry officer, replaced Smith; he made no design changes and pushed ahead vigorously with the existing construction plans.[29]

In mid-April, Bull began construction of a second fort at Red Bank, near the upper rows of chevaux-de-Frise. The new outpost rested on a bluff directly across the river from Fort Mifflin on Fort Island. Bull expropriated land from Benjamin Whitall's parents, James and Ann Whitall, who owned a 196-acre plantation along the river. The construction site quickly became a hive of activity. When the Whitalls' son Job visited on April 16, he found "3 or 4 hundred soldiers there." With large drafts of labor from South Jersey militia and ample timber in adjacent woodland, Bull made rapid progress, and, while not a military engineer, he made a good job of it. In June, a French artillerist, General Philippe du Coudray, judged that the Red Bank fort—soon to be known as Fort Mercer—featured good construction and neared completion.[30]

The overly large and flawed Billingsport fort, however, remained unfinished. In June, Congress requested that New Jersey send five hundred militia to help the Pennsylvania militia working at Billingsport. Such assistance was not immediately forthcoming. New Jersey militia had their hands full with construction at Red Bank. In late July and August, after completing construction at Red Bank, men from the 1st and 2nd Cumberland, 2nd Salem, and 2nd Gloucester Regiments did perform work at Billingsport. There, under the command of Lieutenant Colonel Josiah Hillman—who had commanded militia at Somerset Court House—they ditched and carpentered to reduce the size of the large fort.[31] It proved an exercise in futility, as Billingsport would never play a critical role in the American river defenses—but that became apparent only later in the year.

In the meantime, the South Jersey militia, including the Gloucestermen, had become inured to war. Many were veteran, if part-time, soldiers; they had been under fire and had learned that redcoats were not invincible. They had experienced the various routines of military life: the drudgery and labor of building defensive works, the boring periods of guard duty, vigilance against Loyalist activities, the care of equipment, and the urgency of timely responses to emergencies and raids. Working at Red

Map 6, opposite. Plan and Sections of the Redoubt at Billingsfort and Plan of the Rebel Fort. Drawn by a British engineer, spring 1778. Monsieur John de Kermovan laid out the four-bastioned fort in early July 1776. In July–August 1777, Pennsylvania and New Jersey militia constructed a new wall reducing the size of the fort by two-thirds. The British captured the fort on October 2, 1777, demolished it on October 6, and returned three weeks later to build a redoubt in order to protect their vessels removing the chevaux-de-frise. This redoubt was abandoned on December 10, but on March 22, 1778, the British landed an engineer and eighty West Jersey Volunteers and began construction of the redoubt shown in the plan. (*Library of Congress*)

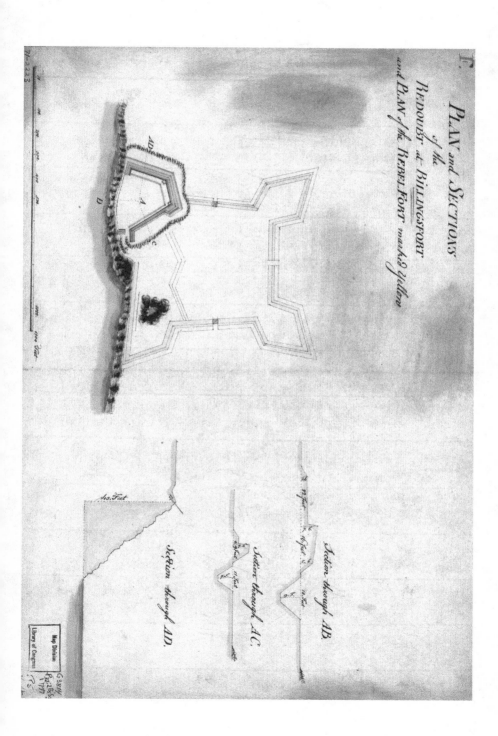

PLAN and SECTIONS
of the
REDOUBT at BILLINGSFORT
and PLAN of the REBEL FORT marked yellow

Section through AB.

Section through A.C.

Section through AD.

Bank and Billingsport had integrated the citizen-soldiers into the defensive network that protected Philadelphia. They had learned much since 1775.

The militia did, however, have problems, including a structural one: one-month enlistments, enlistments that began when a company mustered and not when it reached its service location. Thus, a company from North or Central Jersey would spend at most three weeks in South Jersey before it was time to march home. Even these short enlistments placed a genuine hardship on farmers. In November 1777, some Somerset County privates would march to Gloucester County, fight with Lafayette, and as soon as Cornwallis returned to Philadelphia, bolt for home. Unlike men who disappeared before the fighting, their captain did not consider them deserters.[32]

A second problem was Brigadier General Silas Newcomb of Cumberland County. In March 1777, the New Jersey legislature promoted him to command the South Jersey brigade after Colonels Joseph Ellis and David Potter had declined promotion. Newcomb lacked imagination, decisiveness, and courage and took offense easily. The following October, he failed to defend Fort Billingsport, did nothing at Fort Mercer, and then engaged in petty disputes with his nominal superior, Brigadier General David Forman. Under pressure from the governor and his council, he resigned December 4, 1777. In subsequent correspondence between Governor Livingston and Washington, "Newcomb" became shorthand for incompetent. Fortunately, the very competent Joseph Ellis began filling the void.[33]

The militia's maturation was never more important, for at the end of July 1777, a British fleet with almost eighteen thousand combatants and women had sailed from New York to capture the rebel capital of Philadelphia. The militia would now fight on their home ground.

THREE

Prelude: Two Armies Converge on the Delaware Valley

ON AUGUST 25, 1777, General Sir William Howe, commander in chief of His Majesty's forces in North America, landed his Anglo-German army in Maryland at Head of Elk at the top of Chesapeake Bay.[1] He sought to capture the de facto rebel capital of Philadelphia. Three times Washington unsuccessfully attempted to block the British advance on the city. On September 11, Howe outflanked the Continentals and drove them from the field at Brandywine Creek. Five days later, Washington positioned his army on the hills protecting the best ford over the Schuylkill River, but, just as the British attacked, a violent thunderstorm arose, halting the fighting and forcing Washington to retreat and replace his men's rain-soaked ammunition. Next, the Continentals formed on the river's north bank to stop the enemy from fording it. The British, however, feinted a march to the west toward the important Continental supply depot at Reading. When

Washington shifted his men west, the enemy marched east and forded the Schuylkill. The road to Philadelphia now lay open. On September 26, unopposed, British and Hessian grenadiers paraded into Philadelphia, a band playing "God Save Great George Our King."[2]

While the British now held the largest city in their former colonies, they had no efficient way of supplying it. The rebel chevaux-de-Frise blocked the shipping channel to Philadelphia, and the ordnance at Forts Billingsport, Mifflin, and Mercer provided defensive coverage for the underwater obstructions. On October 5, the British began preparing to lay siege to Fort Mifflin, but progress was slow. Meanwhile, with the Royal Navy unable to supply the city by water, occupied Philadelphia experienced severe shortages and economic inflation. On November 1, Captain John Montrésor, an engineer, noted, "We are just now an army without provisions or Rum, artillery for besieging, scarce any ammunition, no clothing, nor any money."[3] Frustrated, the British reconciled themselves to a long siege. While the British built batteries, the garrisons at Forts Mifflin and Mercer labored to improve their defenses. Howe's efforts to open the Delaware—which meant taking the forts—and the rebel determination to hold them would lead to desperate fighting, which formed the immediate prelude to the marquis de Lafayette's engagement at Gloucester.

PHILADELPHIA: PRIZE OR PRISON?

The rival commanders, George Washington and Sir William Howe, knew that control of the Delaware River could spell the difference between victory or defeat in the ongoing Philadelphia Campaign. Washington hoped to keep the Delaware closed to the Royal Navy, although he had few troops to spare. He had sent large numbers of his best men to reinforce Major General Horatio Gates, then preparing to face an invading British army north of Albany, New York. Still, the rebel general wanted to hold Forts Mifflin and Mercer until the Delaware froze over, which could have made Howe's position in Philadelphia untenable. Howe was desperate to open the river—but what to do? Fort Mifflin stood on Mud (or Fort) Island, difficult to approach by vessel or from Pennsylvania. So the best solution seemed to be an operation on the New Jersey side of the river. If he moved quickly, before the hard-pressed Washington could reinforce the small militia garrisons of Billingsport and Red Bank, Howe might be able to clear the river with a relatively small force.

Howe initially targeted Billingsport, his hope being that seizing the fort would allow the Royal Navy to start clearing the lower chevaux-de-Frise. On October 1, British seamen rowed the troops of the 10th and 42nd Regiments of Foot (the latter the Royal Highlanders)—about 1,100 men—across the river to a landing just above the mouth of Raccoon Creek. Most of the redcoats were battle-hardened veterans, as was their experienced commander, Lieutenant Colonel Thomas Stirling of the 42nd, who had seen plenty of action in the French and Indian War. From Billingsport, Pennsylvania militia Colonel William Bradford, a Philadelphia printer and publisher, observed the crossing and dispatched sixty South Jersey militiamen to keep an eye on the enemy and harass them if they marched.[4] And they did indeed march. Stirling had them moving after breakfast on October 2.

Billingsport was a plum ripe for the picking. Bradford, a competent officer, commanded the garrison. The undermanned garrison, however, comprised only about 100 Pennsylvania militia infantry and 12 artillery men, and perhaps 150 New Jersey militia, including companies from the 1st and 2nd Cumberland Regiments. Several vessels from the Pennsylvania navy, and the Continental navy brig *Andrea Doria*, rode at anchor offshore from the fort.[5] General Silas Newcomb, the senior New Jersey militia officer in the area, was not at Billingsport, preferring the comforts of Woodbury. Early on the morning of October 2, however, he rode to the fort and informed Bradford that "he had a few Militia on the main Road with one Piece of Artillery and was going to harrass the Enemy." Inexperienced Captain Lieutenant Franklin Davenport of Hugg's militia artillery commanded the field piece. Newcomb ordered the Jersey militia in the fort to join him and led them to King's (Salem) Road to find the enemy. Newcomb commanded perhaps 250 militia, and he accomplished little harassing.[6] Bradford was on his own.

South of the Billingsport Road intersection, King's Road crossed two brooks. For regular infantry with artillery support, these would have been tempting locations for making a stand. Fortunately, Newcomb did not try to do so. The odds were not favorable—250 militia versus over 1,000 regulars. Encountering Stirling's men on the road, Newcomb ordered Captain Lieutenant Davenport to open fire with the militia 6-pounder. Davenport fired off a few rounds before suffering a misfire. Not having time to draw the charge, Davenport limbered up the gun and began retreating. Newcomb fought a brief retreating skirmish to the Mantua Creek bridge. There, the militia gave the British a battalion volley and then fled across the bridge. Charles Simpkins of the 1st Cumberland Regiment remembered that "two of our men were wounded and nine taken prisoners." They killed two of the enemy at the bridge, and General Newcomb's horse suffered a wound in the hindquarters.[7]

At the fort, about 8:00 AM, Colonel Bradford heard a "firing . . . which continued but a short time." He ordered his men under arms and sent two officers to locate Newcomb, but Newcomb had retreated to Woodbury. Bradford immediately ordered the fort evacuated. Pennsylvania militia and seamen began loading ammunition and stores on the shipping, spiked the cannons, and set the barracks and bakehouse on fire. After evacuating the stores and men to the boats, Bradford and the captain of the *Andrea Doria* lagged behind to observe. The "Enemy come on so close thro' a corn field that they were not more than 30 yards from us," the colonel remembered, "and began to fire on us before our Boat put off the shore, we returned the fire with 6 muskets we had on board, and a Guard Boat we had with us also fired on them, and all got off, one man only being wounded."[8]

Had Lieutenant Colonel Stirling left a detachment in the ruins of Billingsport and led his main body on King's Road, he could have seized the Red Bank fort the following morning. On October 3, the fort had a minimal garrison, and the militia stationed at Woodbury and Haddonfield were the only additional rebels who could have intervened. Had Stirling done so, the Delaware River could have been open to British shipping early in October. Fortunately for the Revolution, Stirling considered his mission accomplished. HMS *Pearl* sent ashore two naval 12-pounders. With these the garrison could defend British vessels trying to destroy the lower chevaux-de-Frise.[9]

New orders from Howe would have logically sent Stirling north to take Fort Mercer, but Washington intervened. On October 4, he attacked the British just outside Philadelphia at Germantown. The attack failed after a stiff engagement, but a startled Howe recalled the 10th and 42nd Regiments, leaving only the detachment from the 71st Regiment of Foot and some marines at Billingsport.[10] The British missed a golden opportunity, and the Delaware River remained closed. Philadelphia continued as much a prison as a prize.

FORT MERCER, OCTOBER–NOVEMBER 1777

While rebel forces labored to strengthen the works at Fort Mifflin, Washington realized he had to do something about the nearly defenseless Fort Mercer. On October 2, the same day Stirling's troops took Billingsport, the commandant at Fort Mifflin warned Washington about the danger to Fort Mercer and the consequences should the British occupy it.[11] On October 7, the commander in chief reacted, writing Brigadier General James Mitchell Varnum to immediately "detach Col: Green[e]'s and Col: Angel's regiments with their baggage, with orders to throw themselves into the fort at Red-bank upon the Jersey-shore. This important post commands and defends the Chevaux de frize and unless kept in our possession, our vessels of war must quit their station and thereby leave the enemy at liberty to weigh the Chevaux de frize and open the free navigation of the River."[12] These were veteran Rhode Island Continental regiments. He also sent an artillery company and a French artillerist and engineer, Captain Thomas-Antoine de Mauduit du Plessis, to supervise the artillery and improvements to the fort.[13] The Continentals' arrival was a relief to Major William Ellis—a cousin of Joseph Ellis—and the militia garrison. The largest contingent, 154 men, hailed from the western Gloucester townships,[14] and some men may have been there from a Cumberland regiment. Colonel Christopher Greene of the 1st Rhode Island Regiment—the fort's new commander—immediately placed the regulars and militia under the same discipline. Beyond the militia in the garrison, however, Greene wrote Washington on October 14 that he expected little from the militia. "I saw General Newcomb last Evening—He Inform's me that the small number now on duty expects to return Home in a day or Two."[15]

Greene and du Plessis needed to reduce the size of the fort. Greene put the entire garrison on fatigue duty, and his men demolished one of James Whitall's barns to provide lumber. The garrison abandoned the northern two-thirds of the fort. Du Plessis, Comstock, and Ellis directed construction of a new north wall. Continental and militia carpenters framed two east-west timber walls and planked them with siding taken from Whitall's barn. Then the less-skilled men filled the space between the plank walls. At the east end of the wall, on a section of the old rampart, du Plessis constructed a musketry gallery—a *caponnière* (chicken coop). From it, eight soldiers could fire directly along the new wall and ditch. The contraction resulted in a very irregular, five-pointed-star fortification. The angles allowed every section of wall to be protected from an adjacent section.[16]

The Continental reinforcements arrived in a timely manner, for Howe now set his sights on Mercer. Early on October 21, about 1,600 German troops under Colonel Carl Emilius von Donop crossed the Delaware to Cooper's Ferry (modern Camden). A militia guard fired at them and then marched off as mounted militia rode to alert Colonel Ellis. Seeing that the artillery included howitzers, Ellis correctly surmised Donop meant to attack Red Bank. The colonel sent Richard Tice, a fifteen-year-old from Gloucester Township, with a dispatch to Colonel Greene at Red Bank. Other dispatch riders quickly carried news of the Hessian intrusion to Washington's headquarters at Whitemarsh, and the general forwarded the information to John Hancock, president of the Continental Congress. The next day he informed New Jersey Governor Livingston that Howe had thrown "a party over into Jersey at Coopers Ferry, whether with an intent to invest Red Bank or collect Cattle I do not know, but I fear the former."[17]

The Fort Mercer garrison had worked to improve their defenses for days, but Tice's arrival ignited even greater efforts. Colonel Greene ordered the Whitalls' apple orchard cut down to build abatises. Militia and Continentals chopped down the trees, sharpened their branches, and then positioned them around the fort with the sharpened branches pointing out. Commissary officers redoubled their efforts to collect provisions for Forts Mercer and Mifflin.[18] The garrison brought their horses into the fort, and the soldiers appropriated sheep from James Whitall and his neighbor, Joseph Lowe, and herded them into the fort. Work on the defenses continued right up to the appearance of the Hessians.[19] Arriving concomitantly with the Hessians, the 2nd Rhode Island Regiment landed and climbed the bluff to defend the fort. These men spent the previous two and a half days under fire at Fort Mifflin. According to Sergeant Jeremiah Greenman, they "had scarce an opportunity to git into the Fort, before a Flag came to Colo. Green."[20] With the flag came Colonel Donop's demand that the garrison surrender.

With the Rhode Islanders from Fort Mifflin approaching Red Bank, Greene felt confident that he had enough Continentals, and he discharged the militia. They exited the south gate and crossed Woodbury Creek on the tide dam, all except adventurous Jonas Cattell and his friend, Ben Haines. They climbed an ash tree in James Whitall's meadow "to watch the progress of events." Earlier, other militia detachments dismantled the bridges on King's Road between Haddonfield and Woodbury. They had taken up the deck plank of the Great Timber Creek bridge and were demolishing the bridge over the King's Run at Albertson's milldam when warned of the Hessians' approach.[21]

The Hessians appeared before Fort Mercer on the afternoon of October 22, with a Philadelphia butcher, who knew the area, and Dick Ellis, the escaped slave of Colonel Ellis, who certainly knew the area, guiding the invaders.[22] Donop's officers at the

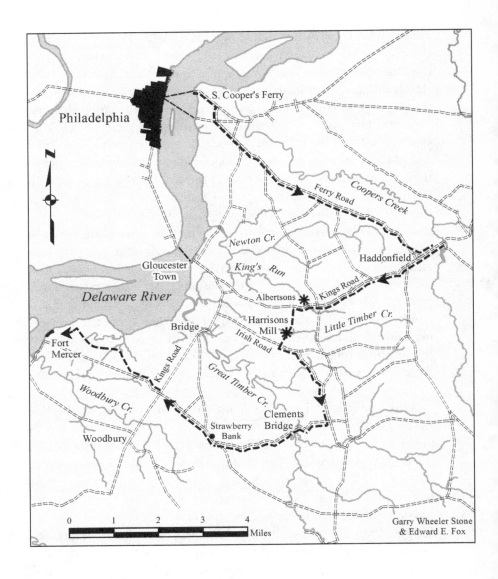

Map 7. The Hessian march from Cooper's Ferry to Fort Mercer. The Hessian march route is based on an anonymous map at the Library of Congress, "Draft of roads in New Jersey." The map clearly depicts Donop's detachment crossing Little Timber Creek on Captain Harrison's mill dam. The map is neither signed nor dated, but Edward Fox has identified it as the work of General John Calwalader, and it probably dates from early November 1777.

front of the column glimpsed Fort Mercer a little before 1:00 PM.[23] The count sent a parley flag to the fort asking for its surrender, and, when Greene politely refused, Donop prepared to attack, directing his men to make fascines—bundles of brush with which to fill up the ditch. Then, after a twenty-minute artillery barrage, Donop attacked in three directions. The battalion attacking from the south, having to struggle through only a single abatis, had the most success, one soldier reaching an embrasure before being killed. The other two attacking battalions poured over the walls of the abandoned portion of the fort only to find themselves in a death trap—cannonaded from the fort and gunboats in the Delaware. Continental men, under the cover of the fort's walls, shot down the Hessians struggling through the double abatis. Few Hessians made it to the ditch.[24]

Forty to forty-five minutes after the assault began, it collapsed. Eighty-two Germans lay dead or mortally wounded, including Donop. An additional 228 suffered wounds. The Hessians lost sixty more to capture or desertion. Greene's command lost only fourteen killed in action and twenty-three wounded. In addition, the following day, two British men-of-war, the 64-gun *Augusta* and the 14-gun *Merlin*, which had worked upriver to support the attacks on Mifflin and Mercer, grounded, burned, and exploded.[25] For the rebels, it provided a solid and resounding victory.

While the able-bodied Hessians and some of their wounded made it back to Philadelphia, the two guides provided by General Howe did not. Had they prematurely celebrated a Hessian victory? The next day, they languished as prisoners in the fort. Captain William Tew, 2nd Rhode Island, took Ellis with him as they investigated the rumor that the Hessians had abandoned some of their field artillery, but found none. On October 31, Greene charged the two guides with treason and had them court-martialed. They were convicted and ordered hanged on November 1. That evening, soldiers buried their remains under the gallows.[26]

A RACE FOR REINFORCEMENTS

Despite the bloody setback at Fort Mercer, the British had no choice but to continue their efforts to open the river. As the

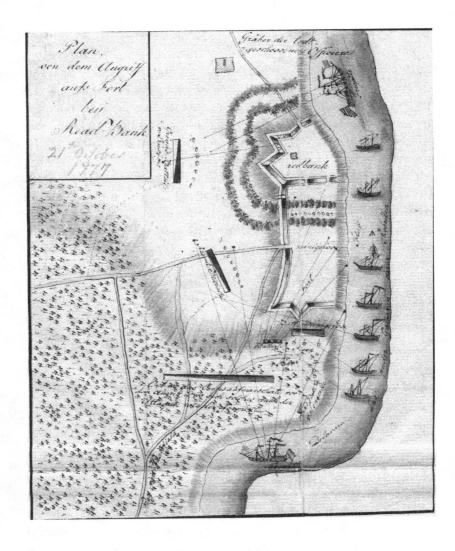

Map 8. *Plan, von dem Angriff aufs Fort bei Read Bank.* Captain Johann Ewald's careful rendering of the attack on Fort Mercer locates the artillery, attacking battalions, and the reserves. The lines of circles in front of the Hessian battalions represent men carrying fascines. In the river, rebel ships and gunboats cannonade the Hessians. Ewald's only major mistake is showing a double abatis around the entire fort. (*Joseph Tustin Papers, Harvey A. Andruss Library, Bloomsburg University, Bloomsburg, PA*)

British had been frustrated in New Jersey, their attention shifted to Fort Mifflin. The British had doggedly constructed artillery positions in the marshes opposite Mud Island, their goal being to bring heavy guns to bear on Fort Mifflin. After weeks of labor, the batteries stood ready, and on November 10, the British began their bombardment. "We opened our Batteries against Mud Island Fort," Captain Montresor wrote, "the whole consisting of two 32 pounders, six 24 pounders Iron, one 18 pounder, two 8 inch Howitzers, two 8 inch mortars, and one 13 inch mortar."[27] The British gunners "much injured" the blockhouses—dismounting several of their guns—shattered a range of barracks, and mowed down sections of palisades. By the thirteenth, the blockhouses consisted of little more than heaps of timber. Work parties of Continentals and militia had to rebuild sections of palisades every night. More and more of the fort's artillery was dismounted. For a time, adverse winds and tides held at bay two British battery vessels, the *Vigilant* and the *Fury*, but on November 15, they moved into position alongside the fort.[28] The first broadside from the *Vigilant*'s 24-pounders leveled the ruins of a blockhouse. The cannonade continued all afternoon, turning Fort Mifflin into a smoking shambles. That night the garrison set the ruined barracks on fire and boarded rowboats with muffled oars for Fort Mercer at Red Bank. When Captain Francis Downman of the Royal Artillery inspected the ruins in the morning, he found a dreadful sight. "It is in such a battered situation that it is past describing. In almost every place you see blood and brains dashed about."[29]

American control of the Delaware now hinged on holding Fort Mercer. At the rebel camp at Whitemarsh, Washington wrote emphatically on the point: "As the keeping possession of Red Bank," he wrote Henry Laurens in Congress, "and thereby still preventing the Enemy from weighing the Chevaux de frize before the Frost obliges their Ships to quit the River, has become a matter of the greatest importance." He decided to send a delegation of generals, Arthur St. Clair, Henry Knox, and the Baron de Kalb, "to endeavour to form a Judgment of the most probable means of securing it."[30] There was no time to waste.

Howe focused on Red Bank as well, and this time he decided on a bolder plan to deal with the troublesome American fort. He would send a larger force—some 4,250 men—under an aggressive but wiser commander: Charles, Lord Cornwallis.[31] On November 17, the first redcoats landed south of Billingsport. The remainder disembarked on the eighteenth, and on the nineteenth they began preparations for their march on Fort Mercer. As an officer reconnoitered the route, a brief skirmish occurred with some militiamen, but no serious fighting developed. Rumors swirled that the American forces had evacuated from Fort Mercer. That night, two companies of light infantry landed below the rebel batteries north of Mantua Creek to confirm the evacuation rumor. When a rebel sentry fired on them, they scrambled back into their boats. The next morning, two other companies arrived to reconnoiter the Mantua Creek batteries. They found them empty except for a spiked 24-pounder. The rebels had retreated.[32]

Washington knew the crisis was at hand. He had received multiple reports that Cornwallis had embarked for New Jersey, and he wrote to Varnum, then at Woodbury, that 1,500 to 3,000 enemy had left Philadelphia to "pay you a Visit." The commander in chief also awaited the report from St. Clair, Knox, and de Kalb, and when a message arrived from the generals, Washington quickly reacted.[33] On November 19, he ordered Brigadier General Jedediah Huntington to march his brigade—about one thousand officers and men—to Red Bank. He then ordered Major General Nathanael Greene to New Jersey with his division: the brigades of Peter Muhlenberg and George Weedon, totaling about an additional 2,100 men. No doubt anticipating a major engagement, Washington alerted other units, ordering them to be ready to reinforce Red Bank as well.[34]

Map 9, opposite. Two armies march for Fort Mercer. It was never possible for Greene to arrive at Fort Mercer ahead of Cornwallis. Cornwallis had a day's head start, and Cornwallis had half the distance to travel (30 miles versus 60). While Cornwallis camped two days at Billingsport, Greene had to wait three days at Mount Holly for Glover's Brigade. Only if General Varnum and Colonel Greene had stubbornly defended the fort, could Major General Greene have arrived in time to relieve the garrison.

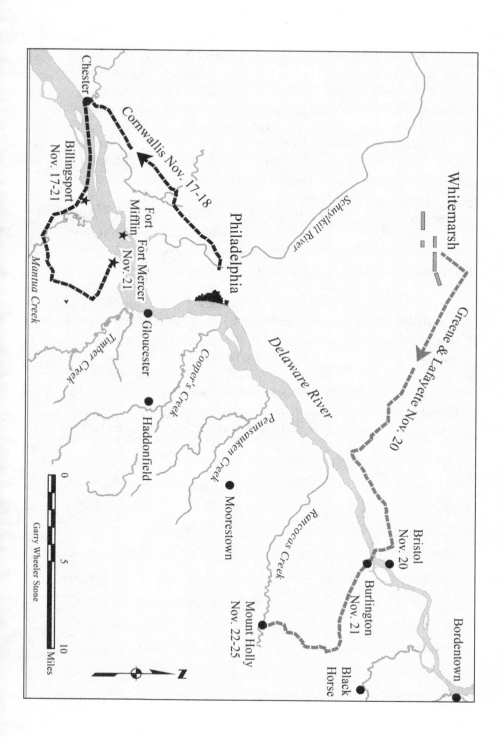

As Greene prepared to leave Whitemarsh, as the reader already knows, an eager young marquis de Lafayette joined his party. Ten weeks earlier, at Brandywine and without a command, Lafayette had suffered a leg wound from a British musket ball. Although not fully healed, he remained active and hoped to see action. "I am just now going from this place with a detachment under Mjor. Gral. Greene," he wrote Henry Laurens. "I hope my wound w'ont be much hurted."[35] He would see action, and soon—but not at Fort Mercer.

On November 20, the British light infantry returned from Mantua Creek and reported that the rebels had retreated, and Cornwallis sent his pioneers and light infantry battalion to King's Road to repair the Mantua Creek Bridge. That evening, the troops saw an explosion at Red Bank. Then flames lit the sky as rebel ships burned at Timber Creek. Colonel Christopher Greene had learned of the British and knew he stood no chance against Cornwallis—and he knew as well that the American relief effort would arrive too late. By the time the British arrived, Greene, Varnum, and their forces had departed. The Americans had evacuated Fort Mercer and Woodbury; the Delaware was open, and for General Howe, Philadelphia, at last, became a prize. The next morning, Cornwallis marched for Woodbury and Fort Mercer.[36]

Figure 1. *Marie-Joseph-Paul-Yves-Roch-Gilbert du Mortier, Marquis de Lafayette* by Charles Willson Peale, oil on canvas, 48.5 x 40 inches, 1780-81. George Washington commissioned this portrait of his surrogate son for Mount Vernon. The painting descended in the Washington family until George Washington Custis Lee presented it to Washington and Lee University in 1897. (*Washington and Lee University*)

Figure 2. *George Washington at Princeton* by Charles Willson Peale, oil on canvas, 94 x 59 inches, 1781. Lafayette met the commander-in-chief at a dinner party in Philadelphia on July 31, 1777—"Although he was surrounded by officers and citizens, the majesty of his figure and his height were unmistakable." This is one of several copies of the almost eight-foot high painting the Pennsylvania Supreme Executive Council commissioned in 1779 for the Pennsylvania State House (Independence Hall). (*Yale University Art Gallery*)

Figure 3. *William Livingston*, an engraving by Albert Rosenthal after a portrait by John Wollaston. New Jersey's wartime governor, Livingston was an able ally of George Washington, continually trying to rally New Jersey's citizens and legislature to do more to defeat Great Britain. A Presbyterian, he saw issues starkly—right versus wrong. Loyalists were "Unnatural Traitors." He wrote Washington that "A Tory is an incorrigible Animal. And nothing but the Extinction of Life, will extinguish his Malevolence against Liberty." In March 1777, Livingston's attorney general prosecuted two Gloucester County Quaker leaders for treason—they refused to swear allegiance to the new rebel government. While they were clearly guilty, the more tolerant Gloucester County court merely fined the men token amounts, five shillings each. (*New York Public Library*)

Figure 4. *Benjamin Franklin* by Charles Willson Peale, oil on canvas, 23.25 x 19 inches, 1785. It was Franklin, famous scientist and brilliant promoter, who inflated the skirmish on the King's Road into the "Battle of Gloucester." Franklin had joined the American delegation to Versailles in December 1776. During the summer of 1779, while Lafayette was in Le Havre with French troops poised to invade England, Franklin worked with Lafayette's cutler on the design of the sword that the Continental Congress had ordered for Lafayette. When Lafayette's cutler inquired how to title the vignettes engraved on the hilt, Franklin wrote back "Retreat of Barren Hill," "Battle of Monmouth," "Retreat of Rhode Island," and "Battle of Gloucester." (*Pennsylvania Academy of Fine Arts*)

Figure 5. *Colonel Christopher Greene* by James Sullivan Lincoln, oil on canvas, 35 x 28 inches, 1863, copying a now lost portrait. Colonel Greene had a distinguished record prior to October 1777—lieutenant in the Kentish Guards in 1774, promoted to major and captured in the attack on Quebec in 1775, and after his exchange, promoted to command of the 1st Rhode Island Regiment. His decisive leadership at Fort Mercer in October 1777 led Congress to award him a sword. However, due to lack of funds, Congress only authorized the acquisition of the sword in 1785, four years after Greene's death. Fabricated by Paris *fourbisseur* Liger, in 1786, Henry Knox, Secretary of War, presented the silver-hilted dress sword to Greene's eldest son. (*Brown University*)

Figure 6. *Colonel Thomas-Antoine, Chevalier de Mauduit du Plessis*, memorial print, circa 1791. Du Plessis was a talented artillerist who fought bravely for the American Revolution only to die in the chaos of the French Revolution. A lieutenant in the French artillery, du Plessis arrived in America in March 1777. He fought at Brandywine, Germantown, Fort Mercer, and Monmouth. In January 1779, with Lafayette, du Plessis returned to France and was appointed a captain in the French artillery. Promoted, in 1787, he was sent to the colony of Haiti to command the Port-au-Prince Regiment. In 1791, he was killed while defending the governor during a mutiny instigated by reactionary white planters. (*Library of Congress*)

Figure 7. *Major General Nathanael Greene* by Charles Willson Peale, oil on canvas, 22.75 x 18.5 inches, 1783. A brilliant military and political thinker, Greene was the officer Washington wanted to succeed him as commander-in-chief should something happen to Washington. Greene was one of the many officers charmed by Lafayette. November 20, 1777, on the trip from Whitemarsh to New Jersey, Greene wrote his wife, Kitty, that, "The Marquis of L[a]F[a]yette is in company with me. He has left a young wife and a fine fortune of 14,000 pounds Sterling per annum to come and engage in the cause of liberty. This is a noble enthusia[s]m. He is a most sweet temper[e]d young gentleman." (*Independence National Historical Park*)

Figure 8. *General Richard Butler*, miniature portrait by John Trumbull, 3 3/4 x 2 7/8 inches, 1790. Trumbull painted General Butler dressed in a fringed hunting shirt, a symbol of Butler's career as a frontier trader, Indian agent, and light infantry commander. Butler's energy, initiative, and fearless pursuit of adventure made him a successful army officer. Repeatedly, he was given special assignments: in Morgan's Rifle Corps, leading "picked men" at the Battle of Monmouth, at the storming of Stony Point, and at the siege of Yorktown. On November 19, 1777, Colonel Butler, Major Morris, and 170 men were detached from the Rifle Corps to join the detachment sent to relieve Fort Mercer. (*Yale University Art Gallery*)

Figure 9. *General Charles Armand Tuffin, the Marquis de la Rouërie*, engraving after a painting by Charles Willson Peale. "Colonel Armand" was a French cavalry officer who, arriving in America in April 1777, made a favorable impression on Congressional delegates and was immediately commissioned a colonel. As Washington and the marquis left the Continental Army in late 1783, Washington wrote a warm letter of thanks to Armand, complimenting him on his "great zeal, intelligence & bravery," at Short Hills, Head of Elk, Brandywine, Whitemarsh, with Lafayette in New Jersey, and at Yorktown. Above all, Washington complimented Armand on his "very handsome partisan stroke" in Westchester County, New York, where the marquis and his corps penetrated deep into enemy territory to capture the major commanding the Loyalist Westchester Militia. (*New York Public Library*)

Figure 10. *Lieutenant Colonel Edmund Brice*, miniature by Charles Willson Peale or Edmund Brice, oil on ivory, 1 1/2 x 1 3/16 inches, ca. 1783. Edmund Brice was born into a prominent Maryland family. His family's wealth provided Edmund with a privileged childhood that included music and art lessons. In 1772 he sailed to England with a letter of introduction to the expatriate Pennsylvania artist Benjamin West. In London, Brice studied with West and was part of a community that included another Marylander, William Carmichael. In early summer 1776, Carmichael moved to France where he became secretary to the American agent, Silas Deane. In late February 1777, Brice received a letter from Carmichael inviting him to hurry to Paris to take "employment" with "gentlemen" (no names were mentioned, as the British were opening Americans' letters). The gentlemen were Baron de Kalb and Lafayette, and Brice became one of Lafayette's aides-de-camp. Just before *La Victoire* sailed for America, the marquis wrote Carmichael "Thank you very much for giving me Mr. Brice, I like him very much, and he is popular with everyone." (*Frick Art Reference Library*)

Figure 11. *Brigadier General James Mitchell Varnum* by Charles Willson Peale, oil on canvas, 23 x 19 inches, 1804, copying a now lost portrait by Peale. A Rhode Island lawyer, Varnum was the first captain of the Kentish Guards, then in May 1775, commissioned colonel of a regiment (later the 1st Rhode Island), and in 1776 promoted to brigadier commanding Rhode Island and Connecticut troops. Arriving at Woodbury, November 2, 1777, he initially did well, harassing the British navy with heavy field pieces and rotating men in and out of Fort Mifflin. But when threatened by the British army, he did nothing to oppose their landing or their crossing of Great Mantua Creek. On November 19, when the garrison of Fort Mercer began to panic, Varnum failed to steady them. Instead, he evacuated the fort and marched his brigade to Mount Holly in a "Precipitate retreat." (*Independence National Historical Park*)

Figure 12. *Jäger Corps*, 1784, hand-colored engraving by J. H. Carl and J. C. Muller. From left to right: Officer, sergeant, horn player, and private. (*Anne S. K. Brown Military Collection, Brown University Library*)

Figure 13, Memorial Stone. "In Memory of David Mulford Lieutenant of the Greenwich Militia, who fell in a skirmish with the Hessians near Haddonfield in the State of New Jersey in the Year 1777, Aged 29 Years." Old Cohansey Baptist Cemetery, Sheppards Mill, Cumberland County, New Jersey. David Mulford (1748–1777), carpenter, was one of the willing soldiers who gave the New Jersey militia its esprit. He joined the Greenwich militia in 1775, was a second lieutenant in the West Cumberland company that marched to New York under Colonel Newcomb in 1776, and in November 1777, he marched to Haddonfield with Captain John Barker. He is buried in an unmarked grave in Haddonfield. (*Photograph by Eric Stephenson*)

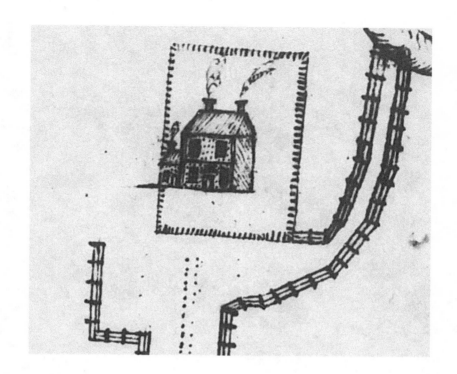

Figure 14. Widow Elizabeth Mickle's home, "Mickle Grove," King's Run, detail from a 1772 survey by Samuel Mickle. John Mickle, Esquire, had been a prosperous yeoman farming 238 acres with the help of servants and slaves. He had been sheriff, 1751–1753. In 1779, Mrs. Mickle had two boarders: Franklin Davenport, attorney, and Israel Morris, Continental Army Assistant Commissary. The front door of Mrs. Mickle's home opened into the dining room. To the right was the parlor (sitting room/master bedroom), to the left the one-story and loft kitchen. Above the dining room and parlor were bed chambers and above them another loft. The surveyor depicted the house, yards, and garden surrounded by a picket fence. To the right of the house, a post-and-rail fenced lane leads to the landing on the King's Run. Many New Jersey families lived in dwellings no larger than the Mickles' kitchen. The house has since been demolished. (Camden County Historical Society)

Figure 15. Colonel Joseph Ellis's Gloucester Town home in 1849, from James Fuller Queen, *House and Factories as Seen on the Edge of a Community*. The residents of this dwelling lived only 230 yards from the courthouse. Matthew Medcalf, sheriff 1701–1710, built the left side (river front) about 1690–1700 as a kitchen and parlor dwelling. His son, Jacob Medcalf, sheriff 1733–36, may have constructed the gambrel-roofed wing. Its south-facing shed porch ("piazza") was a convenient place for household chores. Colonel Ellis was sheriff, 1775–79. Lieutenant General Charles, Lord Cornwallis made Ellis's house his headquarters, November 25–27, 1777. At some time that month, a round shot smashed through the roof of the home. It was demolished in 1882. (*Library of Congress*)

Figure 16. Judge Samuel Harrison's home, Gloucester Town. Judge Harrison's dwelling may have been the largest home in 1777 Gloucester Town Township, and it was a model for several of his cousins' houses. The house was constructed in three stages, with the 1756 two-story brick portion replacing the original wood building. Note the date 1756 in the brickwork. An earlier, one-story brick addition is barely visible to the right. The 1756 section's front door opened into a large dining room, behind which was a parlor. A corner stair in the parlor led to the second-floor chambers. The cove cornice once extended across the gable. It was demolished in 1941. (*Gloucester City Historical Society*)

Figure 17. Captain William Harrison's house, Little Timber Creek, photographed in March 1937 by Nathaniel R. Ewan for the Historic American Building Survey (HABS). Like his uncle Samuel's 1756 dwelling, this structure evolved in three stages, the two-story 1764 portion replacing the original wood dwelling. Earlier, the wood dwelling was improved by the one-story brick wing, probably a dining room. The wing was enlarged in 1764, converted to a kitchen, and enlarged again in the late nineteenth or early twentieth century. The porch is early twentieth century. In 1783, the sheriff advertised the house as "elegant." The New Jersey Department of Transportation demolished the house on March 3, 2017. Their action culminated a fourteen-year effort to evade their responsibilities under the Historic Preservation Act of 1966. While the HABS draftsmen carefully recorded the details of the 1764 structure, the evolution of the kitchen is now lost. NJDOT staff refused to allow Camden County consultants to examine the building or to collect timber samples for dendrochronology (tree-ring dating). (*Library of Congress*)

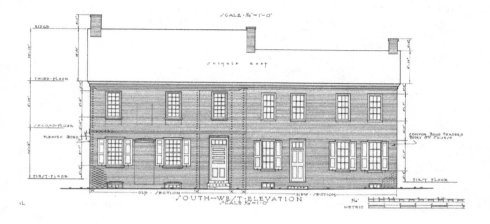

Figure 18. Colonel Joseph Hugg House, 1760s, 1782, and nineteenth-century, Great Timber Creek. Measured and drawn, March and April 1936, rendering by Otto Pahl, HABS. The original wood house became the kitchen wing when Joseph Hugg added a two-story brick addition in the early 1760s (left part of drawing). The brick addition had a centered door (see seams in brickwork) opening into the dining room. Behind the dining room was a parlor, and on the second floor were chambers. Hugg was a conspicuous Whig—clerk of the Committee of Observation, clerk of the County Court, and a Continental Army commissary. The house was occupied by the British Light Infantry, November 22–24, 1777. When they marched to Gloucester Town on November 25, the house burned. About 1778, Hugg constructed a frame house a short distance to the right of the burned-out walls of their former home. Then in 1782, he reconstructed the 1760s house, raising the ceiling of the 2nd floor, changing the fenestration, and extending the house to meet the circa 1778 frame building. The new space provided room for an entrance lobby and stair. Hugg's rebuilt home may have been the first in the Town of Gloucester where the front door did not open into a principal room. The circa 1778 frame dwelling became a kitchen wing, only to be replaced in the nineteenth century by the large brick service wing shown in the drawing (right side). It has since been demolished. (*Library of Congress*)

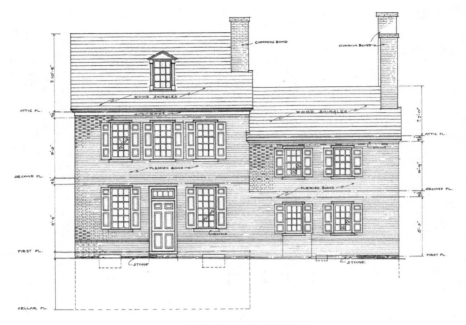

WEST ELEVATION.

Figure 19. Captain Samuel Hugg House, 1768, Great Timber Creek, drawn by H. E. Eichner, June 1936, HABS. Samuel Hugg married Mary Collins in 1764 and they probably began farming their plantation on Great Timber Creek at that time. Four years later, they replaced the old wooden house with this brick dwelling. It was smaller than Judge Harrison's home, but nicely finished with an elegantly paneled fireplace wall in the dining room. The large second-floor parlor was almost as well finished as the dining room. This may have been the first dwelling in the Town of Gloucester to have had a second-story parlor. Hugg was an artillery captain, a light horseman in the 2nd Gloucester troop, and a part-time Continental army commissary. According to family tradition, the party of men who burned his brother Joseph's home were on their way to torch Samuel Hugg's buildings when one of the Hugg's enslaved laborers warned them that militia were waiting in ambush. The house has since been demolished. (*Library of Congress*)

Figure 20. Lafayette's Golden Battle Sword, *"Epéé Dor a Bataille,"* fabricated by Claude-Raymond Liger and drawn by Dr. Jules Cloquet in 1835. The drawing shows the decoration of the grip, pommel, and knuckle bow of the sword presented to Lafayette by Congress. The two leaves of the guard (or shell) are at the bottom of the drawing. Their decoration is not visible as they are perpendicular to the blade and the viewer. Note sword cutler Liger's wording and misspelling of *épeé d'or a bataille.* (*Jules Cloquet,* Recollections of the Private Life of General Lafayette, *New York: Leavitt, Lord & Co., 1836, 2:9, courtesy Lafayette College*)

Figure 21. "The affair at Gloucester," design rendering. The marquis and his aides lead the troops driving the enemy from the battlefield. This is one of four scenes decorating the sword guard. (*National Archives, Papers of the Continental Congress, Item 59, [Miscellaneous Papers, 1770-1789], 1:38*)

Figure 22. "Battle of Gloucester," portion of the sword guard as named by Benjamin Franklin, fabricated by Claude-Raymond Liger and drawn by Dr. Jules Cloquet in 1835. (*Jules Cloquet*, Recollections of the Private Life of General Lafayette, *New York: Leavitt, Lord & Co., 1836, 2:9, courtesy Lafayette College*)

FOUR

Battle: Lafayette's "Little Event"

ON THE TWENTY-FIRST, drums woke the Crown's troops at 5:00 AM. An hour later, the British and German soldiers began marching toward the Mantua Creek bridge.[1] Engineer Archibald Robertson had warned Cornwallis that the bridge was defensible, but he found it abandoned. There he posted troops to "keep up the Communication with Billingsport and to Collect Cattle." The rest of the army marched north on King's Road to Woodbury. There most encamped in a defensive arc around the village. Part of the light infantry reconnoitered, finding the ruins of Fort Mercer deserted and the Timber Creek bridge "Broke up." At Woodbury, the troops were warned not to wander "because of the rebels."[2]

There were indeed rebels, although Cornwallis did not know how many or their exact location. He had his officers post pickets and gather local intelligence. At Fort Mercer, the troops salvaged munitions and provisions, and then began leveling the ramparts.

Other troops foraged—giving Gloucester County its first real taste of war. At the same time, Nathanael Greene, too late to save Mercer, cautiously moved toward Gloucester Town and tried to learn what he could of Cornwallis's dispositions and intentions. What he discovered would send Lafayette into action as a troop commander for the first time.

OCCUPATION

The British occupation brought chaos to Woodbury as soldiers plundered and the army foraged. Job Whitall, farmer, butcher, and meat packer, recorded his family's losses in his diary. Over four days, from November 21–24, redcoats initially took two of his horses and ransacked their home, taking "bread, pyes, milk, chees, meet, dishes, cups, spoons & then took shirts, sheets, Blankets, coverleds, stockings, Breeches, a lite Broadax and drove our catle."[3] The next day they returned to take milk and potatoes and steal a pig; a British quartermaster or engineer then made off with the wheels and undercarriage of a wagon. When Whitall visited an uncle's home he found another ransacked house—doors broken down and desk drawers forced. In the cellar, the British soldiers broke open a cask of Job Whitall's sugar and took most of its contents. While Job was there, soldiers came and took ten of his father's sheep and four of a neighbor's. Returning home, he found soldiers loading as much hay as they could on horses. On the twenty-fourth, the army left and Whitall checked his smokehouse on the other side of Woodbury. They had taken his bacon, barrel staves, and "near a thousand feet of Boards."[4]

It appears that Cornwallis's foraging was more of a plundering than a well-conducted forage. The Whitalls embraced Quaker pacifism and endured fines for not joining the militia, but no British officer offered to pay for their cattle, wagon gears, or hay. Enough complaints of the Gloucester County plundering reached Philadelphia that—probably with pressure from Howe—Cornwallis announced that all owners of foraged cattle could come to Philadelphia, claim them, and be paid full value. While some Philadelphia Loyalists likely appreciated this proclamation, and it read well in English papers, it offered little consolation to

South Jersey farmers since rebel authorities had ruled traveling to Philadelphia illegal.[5]

While some soldiers plundered, others worked. The Fort Mercer garrison's retreating to Mount Holly on the twenty-first allowed Cornwallis to bring up the 7th and 63rd Regiments from Mantua Bridge. He dispatched the 26th and 63rd Regiments to Fort Mercer to demolish the fortifications, while the 7th Regiment replaced the 1st Light Infantry Battalion in maintaining the Woodbury perimeter. The light infantry returned to the broken bridge at Great Timber Creek. Five of its thirteen companies crossed the creek in two small boats to "Cover the Workmen employ'd in repairing it."[6]

Just east of the bridge stood the plantation of County Clerk Joseph Hugg, a Continental army commissary. Probably, the British officers moved into the Hugg dwelling while their men scouted for comfortable places to bed down in the outbuildings. Others, with their thoughts on supper, attacked the Hugg poultry yard.[7] Late on the twenty-second, events turned nasty. Captain Julius Stirke of the light infantry's 10th Company wrote in his journal, "In the Evening small party's of the Rebels appear'd and begun to be troublesome firing on us from a railing on the Other side of a small swamp, from which we soon drove them, but with the loss of 2 men of the 5th light Company kill'd, and a man of ye 4th Company Wounded."[8] The British carried their casualties to the Hugg dwelling. Two died and their comrades buried them in an adjacent field. The "Rebels" driven back included militia from Burlington, Cumberland, and Gloucester Counties, and they continued to hover near and occasionally alarm British positions.[9]

At daybreak on the twenty-fifth, Cornwallis reunited his army, crossed Little Timber Creek, and marched into Gloucester Town. Behind him, smoldering ruins marked the locations of Joseph Hugg's and Israel Morris's dwellings. In Gloucester Town, the troops began the tedious work of preparing to recross the Delaware to Philadelphia. With only two wharves, the work of embarking foraged cattle, army horses, baggage, and artillery would not be completed until noon on the twenty-seventh. Simultaneously, sailors ferried troops across the river on flatboats. At six in the evening, the 10-gun *Viper* anchored near the shore. There, its 3-pounder guns joined the massive 24-pounders of *Vigilant* in protecting the embarkation from rebel attack.[10] And attack was a possibility, as rebel forces patrolled the British perimeter.

COMBATANTS

The New Jersey Militia

The need for more militia in South Jersey became urgent—urgent enough that at the beginning of November 1777, New Jersey's militia commander, Major General Philemon Dickinson, sent reinforcements from Elizabeth Town south to Fort Mercer. Dickinson's dispatch of troops revealed his concern about the military situation in South Jersey, as he was planning a militia attack on Staten Island. On November 8, Washington urged Governor Livingston to "embody" more at Haddonfield. The following week, General Dickinson wrote Washington that about five hundred more militia were on the march to Red Bank.[11] Present for the skirmish were large contingents from Morris and Burlington Counties, at least token numbers from Essex, Middlesex, and Monmouth Counties, and several companies from Somerset County.

Unsurprisingly, the largest body of men present hailed from the three Gloucester County regiments, but the other southern counties had men in Gloucester County. Salem was well represented, Cumberland had one company there, and the tiny Cape May regiment—it had only four companies—sent fifty men.

The militia assembling at Haddonfield, Woodbury, and Red Bank comprised a diverse group, the men varying from eager warriors to the very reluctant. For some, this would be their first tour, while others had served multiple tours and seen more combat than recent recruits in the Continental army. Their equipment varied: some men carried civilian long fowlers (shotguns) with their cartridges in a coat pocket, while others, fully equipped, carried military muskets, bayonets, and cartridge boxes. Some officers wore uniforms. The best-equipped men may have been from merchant Richard Somers's 3rd Gloucester Regiment. He had the West Indies contacts needed to purchase arms. In 1776, he had ordered one hundred bayonets from a master smith—one of his company commanders—and had salvaged more arms from the wreck of the *Rebecca and Francis*. Cumberland County's 1st Regiment represented the more typical unit. In 1780, it included 477 rank and file for which the private and public arms available consisted of 402 guns, 152 bayonets, and 230 cartridge boxes. When men not owning muskets mustered, their captains issued them public arms, which were checked back in at the end of the tour.[12]

Joseph Ellis, high sheriff of Gloucester County and colonel of its 2nd Regiment, commanded these men, and—since the disgrace of General Newcomb—Ellis served as de facto commander of the South Jersey brigade. It appears Colonel Joseph Haight of Burlington County was second in command. Haight brought the second-largest party of infantry—over two hundred men—and a troop of horse to Haddonfield.

These men represent half of those who would march with Lafayette on November 25—drums beating and officers recognizable in their uniforms. The other half consisted of men from Colonel Daniel Morgan's Rifle Corps.

Daniel Morgan's Rifle Corps
Our image of the Revolutionary War rifleman—lean, tough, fringed hunting shirt, powder horn, and bullet pouch—has much of its origin in Colonel Daniel Morgan's Rifle Corps. About 170 men from this corps arrived in Haddonfield on November 22. These men made up the third of the corps whose bodies and shoes could march after their 260-mile trek from the Saratoga battlefield to Whitemarsh. We do not know to which of the corps's eight companies these men belonged, nor which company officers accompanied them.[13]

The enlisted men of the Rifle Corps had been recruited from Pennsylvania's and Virginia's frontier counties. There, hunting and trapping remained important sources of income, and militia service had provided combat experience. These men had access

COUNTY	COMMANDING OFFICER	MEN	EST. MEN
Morris	Lt. Col. Hathaway		178
Essex	Capt. Myers		?
Middlesex	Maj. Nixon		35
Monmouth	Lt. Col. Lawrence?		60
Somerset	Lt. Col. Middagh		99
Burlington	Lt. Col. Haight		237
Burlington Horse	Capt. Borden		20
1st Gloucester	Lt. Col. Shute		150
2nd Gloucester	Col. Joseph Ellis	154	
3rd Gloucester	Men from 6 companies		100+
Salem	Capt. Kelly		74
Cumberland	Maj. Foster		28
Cape May	Capt. Stites	50	
AGGREGATE TOTAL			1,185+/-

Table 2. Estimated Number of Militia Serving at Haddonfield under Col. Joseph Ellis during late November 1777. Based on Auditor's Book B.

to rifles manufactured by the German gunsmiths of Pennsylvania and Virginia. Many of these riflemen were tough, self-reliant, and bold. Probably a few had followed men like Daniel Boone and James Knox on "long hunts" into Kentucky. Most were unmarried men in their early twenties.[14]

Colonel Richard Butler was second in command of Morgan's corps and colonel of Pennsylvania's 9th Regiment. He was born in Ireland, and his family immigrated to Lancaster County, Pennsylvania, later moving farther west to Carlisle. Butler's father was a blacksmith and gunsmith and taught the trade to Richard. In 1764, Richard Butler participated in a British military expedition deep into the Ohio Country. After working as a gunsmith in Pittsburgh, Richard and his younger brother, William, became partners in trading with the Ohio Valley Native Americans. Their thirst for adventure carried them as far as the French settlements on the Mississippi. During August 1775–April 1776, Richard Butler became the Continental Congress's agent to the Ohio Valley indigenous people, touring their villages and arranging for a conference near Pittsburgh. In a 1776 report to Congress, Butler warned that war in the Ohio Country would more likely result from crimes white settlers committed than the misdeeds of Native Americans. In July 1776, Butler received a commission as major of the 8th Pennsylvania Regiment, a frontier regiment largely recruited in the Monongahela Valley. On June 7, 1777, Butler became colonel of the 9th Pennsylvania Regiment, but two days later, he entered service with Morgan's Rifle Corps.[15]

The corps's major, Joseph Morris (1732–1778), came from a very different background. Before joining the Continental army, he had kept a tavern near Morristown, New Jersey. Like Morgan and Butler, he was a physically powerful man, rashly brave, and inclined toward the military. He served in the Morris County militia during the French and Indian War, and in 1769 and 1771, he served in the Wyoming Valley during the dispute between Pennsylvania and Connecticut settlers. On May 2, 1775, after the news of Lexington and Concord reached Morris County, officials there created five militia companies, choosing Morris to captain one of them. In November, he became a Continental captain in the 1st New Jersey Regiment, and then Washington promoted him to major, effective January 1, 1777. Morris proved to be an apparently unusually dependable officer, as twice early in 1777, Washington assigned him to deal with New Jersey Loyalists. Chosen major of the Rifle Corps, Morris became known as "Brave Major Morris."[16]

From the creation of the corps during the first two weeks of June 1777, until the British evacuated New Jersey at the end of the month, Morgan's men skirmished with the enemy. Then, on August 17, Morgan received orders sending the corps to join General Horatio Gates's army near Albany, New York. Gates and the Northern Army had been sent there to block an invasion from Canada by General John Burgoyne.[17] Morgan and his men had been dispatched to counter the effects of Burgoyne's Native American allies and Loyalist rangers. They did this and more. Reinforced with two hundred light infantry led by Major Henry

Dearborn, men from the corps reconnoitered, skirmished, and then, on September 19, inflicted heavy casualties on the British army in daylong fighting at Freeman's Farm. The successful pairing of Morgan's riflemen with Dearborn's musket men foreshadowed the pairing of riflemen and bayonet-equipped militia at the Battle of Gloucester.

These hardy frontiersmen were a rough lot, prone to brawling. For the Quakers of Haddonfield, the riflemen proved to be just another 170 unwelcome guests, joining the hundreds of militia already crammed into taverns, barns, stables, vacant dwellings, and the Friends' meetinghouse.[18]

Hessian Jägers

In German, jäger means "hunter," and that describes these men—the gamekeepers for the owners of estates. These men could move silently through the forest to stalk and kill game with their short-barreled rifles. They organized shoots for the owner's friends and arrested poachers. Among the rural population, being a jäger was a prized job, frequently handed from father to son for generations. While probably few head gamekeepers served in the jäger companies, the military pay and accoutrements attracted journeymen and apprentices to the ranks. The military jäger's dark green coats with crimson trim offered a visible improvement over civilian jäger attire.[19]

On January 15, 1776, negotiators from Britain and the German state of Hesse-Cassel signed a treaty of alliance whereby Hesse-Cassel would provide fifteen infantry battalions, two jäger companies, and an artillery detachment to its old ally Britain. The selected Hessian units then marched or boated to German coastal ports where they underwent inspection, swore oaths of allegiance to George III, and boarded transports for America. The first division—including the 1st Jäger Company—arrived in New York harbor in late June. The second division and the 2nd Jäger Company arrived October 22.[20] The jäger riflemen quickly became valued members of the Anglo-German army. Exceptional officers commanded both companies—men intelligent, aggressive, and humane. Captain Johann Ewald, the more famous of the two, commanded the 2nd Company. Intensely ambitious, Ewald advanced his career through military publications beginning in 1774. At the time, however, the German and British officers regarded Captain Carl August von Wrede, commander of the 1st Company—commissioned in 1774 a week before Ewald—equally highly.[21]

British and German officers quickly understood the jägers' value. Requests for more went to the German princes. On June 3, 1777, German reinforcements arrived at New York with replacements for Wrede's and Ewald's casualties, a new company of Hessian jägers, a troop of mounted jägers, and a company of jägers from the German principality of Anspach. More Hessian jägers arrived June 16. Most of the Anspachers possessed forestry skills. The Hessians, however, contained only a few foresters—Hesse-Cassel had no more surplus jägers. The rest were an undisciplined rabble requiring strict discipline from experienced corporals. On June 23, the whole jäger force—about six hundred men—was formed into a corps under Lieutenant Colonel Ludwig Johann Adolf von Wurmb. After late June skirmishing, the Jäger Corps boarded transports, along with the rest of Howe's army, for the voyage to the Chesapeake.[22]

Upon arrival of the British army at the Head of Elk, August 3, 1777, the Jäger Corps disembarked first and led the advance into Delaware and southern Pennsylvania. At Iron Hill, Delaware, part of the Battle of Coochs's Bridge, Howe sent the corps and the 1st Battalion of the British Light Infantry to drive General William Maxwell's rifle-armed light infantry from the hill. Ravines and an unfordable stream blocked the British light infantry advance, but in seven hours of skirmishing, the Jäger Corps drove the Continentals from the hill. At a crucial moment, Wrede's men slung their rifles and attacked with hunting swords.[23] For the remainder of the campaign to take Philadelphia, the jägers continued at the head or flanks of the columns and fought at Brandywine and Germantown. On October 21, the Jäger Corps crossed the Delaware River as part of Colonel Donop's expedition to take Fort Mercer.

On September 27, 1777, transports arrived at New York with two new jäger companies and recruits to replace losses in the Jäger Corps—over four hundred men, including a judge advocate, a provost marshal and assistant, a rifle-maker and assistant, a farrier, and an ambulance driver. A few wives accompanied their husbands. Some men died in the expedition to Forts Clinton and Montgomery, but on October 24, 355 reinforcements for the Jäger Corps embarked at New York as part of General Wilson's reinforcement of Howe's Philadelphia army. The subaltern officers among the jäger reinforcements included some competent men, but the enlisted men proved to be a miserable lot. In a November 30 letter to Landgraf Friedrich, Lieutenant General Wilhelm von Knyphausen described them as largely foreigners looking for free transportation to America, deserting as quickly as possible, robbing civilians, and stealing from fellow soldiers. Captain Ewald characterized them as "deserters from all nations, . . . ruined officers and noblemen, students from all the universities, bankrupts, merchants, and all kinds of adventurers." These recruits made up most of the men that Lafayette confronted November 25, 1777.[24]

THE SKIRMISH WITH THE JÄGER PICKET

The marquis; Majors Brice and Gimat; Captain du Plessis; and Colonels Charles Armand Tuffin, marquis de la Rouërie; and Jean Batiste Joseph, chevalier de Laumoy, rode into Haddonfield after dark on Monday, November 24. Brigadier General George Weedon accompanied them. At Haddonfield, the party sought a place to stay as their first order of business and to arrange for the care of their horses—not an easy task. The town had only forty to fifty families, and militia officers had filled the taverns while their men crowded into the Friends' meetinghouse and the haymows of stables and barns. The marquis may have delegated finding lodging and stabling to Brice and du Plessis while Lafayette and Weedon inquired for Lieutenant Colonel Adam Comstock, Colonel Ellis, or someone who could brief them on the military situation.[25]

Major General Greene arrived in Mount Holly "a stranger to all the lower part of the Jerseys," but he quickly began gathering information from militia and Brigadier General Varnum, and he sent detachments forward to gather more—the Burlington militia to Moorestown and Morgan's riflemen to Haddonfield. Before the end of the twenty-second, Greene had learned of the skirmish that evening on commissary Joseph Hugg's plantation and that the British planned to advance to Haddonfield and cross back to Philadelphia at Cooper's Ferry—a plan canceled as the British learned of Greene's approach. On November 23, Greene sent one of Varnum's officers, Lieutenant Colonel Comstock, 1st Rhode Island, back to Haddonfield to coordinate gathering intelligence. With Comstock, Greene sent a letter to Ellis. The next day, Ellis replied that he had four hundred militia in Haddonfield and one hundred more below Mantua Creek. While Cornwallis had most of his men at Woodbury, his lines extended from Mantua Creek to the neck between Great and Little Timber Creeks. Ellis's succinct and informative letter indicated that he had begun filling the leadership void created through Newcomb's disgrace and Forman's resignation.[26]

At seven o'clock Monday evening, Lafayette and Weedon sat down to write reports to Greene. They had learned a lot since arriving at Haddonfield. Not only had the militia been monitoring enemy activities, but Captain Henry Lee's troopers of the 1st Continental Light Dragoons had captured nine British grenadiers while plundering, prisoners whom Colonel Comstock had interrogated. Most of the enemy bivouacked between Great and Little Timber Creeks. They consisted of about 4,250 infantry, 16 field pieces, and reputedly 100 light horse—although Weedon thought the number of light horse was exaggerated. Lafayette was preparing a detailed listing of the British and Hessian units.[27]

Weedon had just signed his report when a dispatch rider arrived from Mount Holly with an unwelcome message—a brief letter from one of Greene's aides. Greene's detachment would march for Haddonfield in the morning, and Greene "wishes you would be here with the Marquis, if not too much fatigued to night. Should the Ma[r]quis be fatigued the General think he had best join us in the morning." Both men were tired, as Weedon indicated in a postscript to his report. "I have this moment

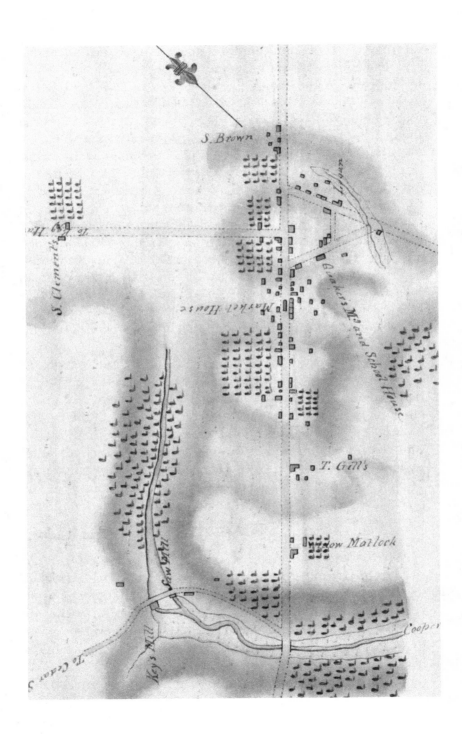

recd your Orders to return. Myself and Horse is so much fatigued that cant get further than Moors Town tonight. Shall join you Early in the morning. G W." While General Weedon, having troops to command, returned to Moorestown, the tired Lafayette had no such responsibilities and remained in Haddonfield. His list of the enemy units has not survived.[28]

Tuesday, November 25, Captain Lee's light dragoons and Ellis's militia were out again, monitoring Cornwallis's detachment as it crossed Little Timber Creek and marched to Gloucester Town, where, by mid-morning, it had encamped. The militia tried to protect local residents by preventing enemy soldiers from venturing outside of their camps to plunder. Captured soldiers also provided intelligence. On the twenty-fifth, Lieutenant Colonel Comstock sent two intelligence reports. A third report, from Lafayette, does not survive.[29]

Comstock wanted information from inside the Gloucester Town encampments. A local militia officer—most likely Colonel Ellis, a Gloucester Town resident—suggested "a smart young woman who had a sister in Gloster." This brave young spy invented a suitable pretext, crossed Little Timber Creek, hiked a mile and a quarter past sentries and through German and British camps to visit her sister, hiked back, and returned to Comstock, having "rec'd no other damage than . . . a Kiss from the Hessian General." The British and Hessians had begun embarking for Philadelphia early in the morning, Cornwallis made his quarters in Colonel Ellis's house, and the "Hessian General" stayed opposite. "She passed many Sentrys before she came to Little Timber Creek Bridge where she passed the last." Comstock expressed concern that the enemy might escape—"I fear they will be too quick for us"—and sent this information to Greene shortly after 12:30 PM.[30]

Map 10, opposite. John Hills, *A Sketch of Haddonfield. West New Jersey County, March 1778*, detail. Hills, a draftsman in the British engineers, illustrates buildings, orchards and woods, roads, and slopes (through shading). He depicts 58 buildings fronting on streets. Some of these were shops and offices. A Scots officer quartered in Haddonfield in March estimated its population as forty families. (*William L. Clements Library, University of Michigan*)

An hour and a half later, he sent off a dispatch rider to Greene with news from interrogating prisoners. A militia scout of Egg Harbor, Galloway, and local men had rounded up seven British soldiers marauding along King's Road. Four of the men had brought three artillery horses (branded "GR"—*Georgius Rex*) on which to pack out their plunder. Just after 3:00 PM, militia arrived with seven captured jägers—several accompanied by their wives. From the prisoners, Comstock learned that the enemy's encampment formed a rough triangle. Artillery companies with pairs of 6-pounders occupied positions on King's Road east and south of the village. The troops would remain at Gloucester Town until the horses and cattle embarked. The soldiers expected to embark tomorrow. The prisoners had not been aware of the Continental soldiers' proximity. Comstock concluded, "I wish your Army was here now for I think they may be supprisd very easy. [. . .] O how I want to give em a Floging before they Leave the Gerseys."[31] A good intelligence officer, Comstock would win no spelling bees.

LAFAYETTE'S RECONNAISSANCE

We know a great deal about Lafayette's afternoon but little about his morning. Did he join militia officers in riding west on King's Road to watch the enemy march into Gloucester Town, or did he accompany Comstock as the lieutenant colonel arranged for the "smart young woman" to venture north on King's Road into the village? On the twenty-sixth, he wrote to Washington that he had reconnoitered "to be acquainted of all the roads and ground arround the ennemy." We do know that the marquis's agenda differed from Comstock's. While the lieutenant colonel collected intelligence for Greene, the marquis reconnoitered looking for a vulnerable unit to attack.[32]

During the afternoon, Lafayette investigated Gloucester Town from the north. His aides and three French officers rode with him. Militia Colonel Ellis would have provided guides from Captain John Stoke's Newton Township militia. Some of Morgan's riflemen gave the party muscle. The following day, Lafayette reported to Washington "that the riflemen had been the whole day running before my horse without eating or taking any rest."[33] From the reconnaissance notes and memories synthesized in Michel Capitaine's map of the skirmish, we know that Lafayette's party made a wide, counterclockwise sweep to observe the British camps from north of Newton Creek.

From Haddonfield, Lafayette's party marched west through the farms along King's Road. A mile from Haddonfield, at young Joseph Hinchman's farm—part of one thousand acres his great-grandfather purchased in 1699—Lafayette turned north on a byway that led between lands of the Redman brothers, Thomas and John (both tracts apparently tenant occupied). A mile farther, they zigged west between the farms of Benjamin Graisbury and David Branson, then zagged north through James Cooper's farm to cross the main branch of Newton Creek. When into Benjamin Thackara's land, they passed Newton Meeting House and its graveyard, the heart of the 1680s New Town settlement. Turning west into Isaac Burrough Sr.'s land, they then crossed Back Creek and marched a narrow road between the woodland of Hannah Cooper and Jacob Stokes—Captain John Stokes's father. Another turn to the west, and Lafayette's party had reached the river road that led from Cooper's Ferry to Gloucester Town.[34]

Like Gloucestertown Township farmers, Newton Township farmers prospered from their proximity to the city and port of Philadelphia. As Lafayette's party marched, the riflemen may have cast hungry eyes at the herds of cattle. Despite foraging by rival armies in 1777–78 and sales to Continental army commissaries and plundered neighbors, in February 1779, the farms of yeomen along Lafayette's route were reasonably well stocked. James Cooper paid a tax for twenty-two cattle (two years old and older), Isaac Burrough Sr., fourteen; Benjamin Thackara, thirteen; Richard Collings (the market gardener), eleven; and Jacob Stokes, thirteen. The assessment identified only Stokes as a significant pork producer, with twenty hogs, his neighbors apparently concentrating on beef, butter, and cheese.[35]

Having reached the river road, Lafayette turned south. A third of a mile later, having passed the lane to Jacob Stokes's farm, the

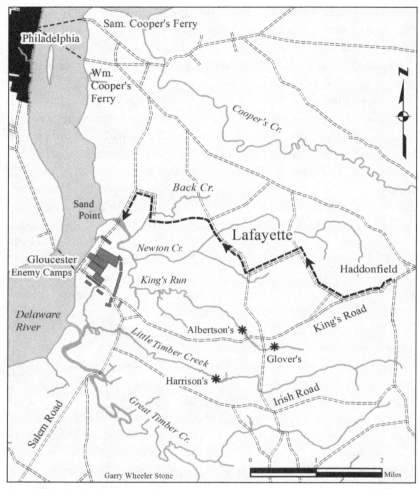

Map 11. Lafayette's Reconnaissance.

reconnaissance party arrived at the mouth of Newton Creek. From Sand Point, Lafayette could see enemy troops being ferried across the river in flatboats, while horse sloops and schooners carried the dragoons' horses and foraged cattle to the ferry wharf on the Pennsylvania side. The Continental officers observed portions of the Gloucester Town encampments. On the opposite shore, west of the dismantled bridge, a British unit held a position on a sand hill. Lafayette sent a rider back to Haddonfield to alert Greene of the enemy's departure. Then the marquis returned to Haddonfield, determined to "annoy" the enemy.[36]

LAFAYETTE'S "LITTLE EVENT"

Back in Haddonfield, Lafayette conferred with Colonels Ellis and Comstock. The marquis learned from them and others that the nearest enemy consisted of a jäger picket of 350 riflemen on the outskirts of Gloucester Town in the triangular intersection of the King's and Gloucestertown Roads. Closer to Haddonfield, the jägers had an outpost where the road crossed the King's Run on Jacob Albertson's milldam. Since mid-afternoon, militia had been harassing the outpost. The jägers looked vulnerable, and Lafayette, eager to engage, sought help from the militia.

Lafayette asked for Ellis's support in an attack on the jägers. Ellis agreed, but he had only limited resources. Many of his men were in the cordon around the enemy encampment. Others stood guard at Mantua Creek and Cooper's Ferry, while still others slept after being on guard during the night. Ellis offered Lafayette about 150 men, and he accepted. Ellis then issued orders, some of which Lieutenant Colonel Haight passed on. Private John Auten heard Haight alert Lieutenant Colonel Derick Middagh and the Somerset County company commanders that they would march in an hour. These officers' men made up detachments from at least six counties—from Somerset in the north to Cumberland in the south. While the ranks may have included some youngsters, many of these men were experienced irregulars, some serving intermittently since December 1775. They had been drilled, many under the tutelage of French and Indian War veterans like Colonel Ellis. Uniforms and other symbols of rank distinguished some company officers and sergeants, and their men marched to the beat of the drum. More importantly, some of the men forming up carried bayonets for their muskets. These were not amateur units. It was almost 2:00 PM. An hour later, they marched, the rifle detachment in the lead, followed by Lafayette's party, light dragoons, and the militia. As they marched, other militia may have joined the column. At a little before 3:00 PM, the column had almost three miles to march before reaching the jäger outpost.[37] Knowing the area intimately, Ellis accompanied the Frenchman, staying in touch with militia videttes (mounted pickets) and keeping abreast of new intelligence. Lafayette was lucky to have him along.

In front of the column, Captain du Plessis led a scout to locate the jägers. Du Plessis—having been stationed at Fort Mercer—had ridden King's Road several times. Behind the scout, at the head of the column, Colonel Richard Butler and Major Joseph Morris led 150 of the 170 Morgan's riflemen who had arrived from Whitemarsh. A few of the detachment, probably those whose shoes had failed during the march from Pennsylvania, stayed in Haddonfield to guard their baggage. (Colonel Morgan remained with the larger part of the corps at Whitemarsh.)[38]

Aides Majors Brice and Gimat, and Colonels Laumoy and Armand rode with Lafayette; Armand was the senior colonel with the detachment (commissioned May 10, 1777). When Washington wrote a farewell letter to him in 1783, he noted Armand's spirited behavior on battlefields "particularly when under the Marqs. de la Fayette & next in command to him in the Jerseys." The light horse consisted of ten troopers from Captain Henry Lee's troop of the 1st Continental Light Dragoons. Lieutenant William Lindsay commanded these troopers, loaned to Lee's 5th Troop from the 3rd Troop. Some militia light horse may have ridden with Lindsay's troopers.[39]

Officers at the front of the militia detachment with Lieutenant Colonel Haight included Captain John Stokes, Newton Township militia, and Captain John Barker and Lieutenant David Mulford, 2nd Cumberland. Part of 7th Company, 3rd Gloucester joined Barker's Cumberland County men. Coastal Galloway Township provided a company-sized unit (men from 3rd Gloucester's 1st and 8th Companies). They had arrived in Haddonfield under Captain George Payne. Payne had returned home to gather more men, leaving the command to Lieutenant John Lucas and Ensign John Tilton. Captain Peter Dubois's men from 2nd Salem also marched near the front. Behind them marched men from Burlington, Somerset, and Middlesex Counties.[40] Lafayette's detachment had only "marched a small distance" when it passed other militiamen escorting seven jäger prisoners. These prisoners arrived in Haddonfield after Colonel Comstock began his three o'clock report to Greene.[41]

A mile and a quarter from Haddonfield, Colonel Ellis sent out flanking parties. One marched north on the road to Atmore's dam before turning west to file through the fields and woods parallel to King's Road. Michel Capitaine's schematic map of the skirmish shows only flanking parties to the north, but Ellis certainly sent men to the south where Irish Road between Little and Great Timber Creeks facilitated movement.

After marching over two miles, the militia heard rifle fire—Morgan's men had engaged the enemy. Adrenaline surged and the men pushed on. As they neared the gunfire, Lieutenant Colonel Haight briefly halted the column. He directed Lieutenant Colonel Middagh to form a rear guard with a third of the men. With the other two-thirds, Haight rushed on to support the Continental riflemen.[42]

Captain Carl August von Wrede's 350-man detachment of the Jäger Corps formed a large picket on the King's Road east of Gloucester Town. Farther east, near the King's Run bridge, Captain Wrede had established a smaller picket of Lieutenant Friedrich Kellerhausen and twenty-six men. A logical posting would have been in or near the home of Mary and Ben Bates; from there Kellerhausen could have watched King's Road and the road from Timber Creek to Cooper's Ferry. When, at about 2:00 PM, militia began harassing Kellerhausen's men, Wrede marched with the entire detachment to the outpost's relief. After crossing the King's Run bridge, Wrede posted a reserve to cover the bridge and the outpost. This reserve consisted of a third of the recruits—perhaps ninety jägers—under Lieutenant Franz Christian von Bodungen. Wrede then arrayed his men to reconnoiter the road and the woods: thirty experienced jägers from Philadelphia in the center, a third of the recruits to the left, and a third to the right. With each group, Wrede posted an experienced officer: Lieutenant George Hermann Heppe on the left and Lieutenant Erich Carl von Hagen to the right. In the center, Ensign Wilhelm Freyenhagen accompanied Captain Wrede. Freyenhagen's diary preserves the only detailed description of the skirmish—although he overestimated the size of Lafayette's detachment. "We barely advanced 100 paces," he wrote, "when the enemy advanced on us in the best order with overwhelming superior numbers. He attacked with the heaviest musket fire, and he was able on the flanks to mortally wound both Lts. Heppe and v. Hagen and force their commands back. Then with force and bravery he stormed the remainder. As we were outflanked on all sides Capt v. Wrede began a retreat."[43]

The skirmish began as American riflemen versus German riflemen. Although the jägers outnumbered Morgan's riflemen more than two to one, it was a lopsided fight. The jäger recruits—90 percent of the detachment—had no experience in bush fighting and little firearms training. Later, back in Philadelphia, Captain Wrede reported to Lieutenant General Knyphausen that the major factors in the jägers' defeat were the recruits' "inexperience in maneuvers and lack of promptitude in loading." The Americans duplicated their Saratoga tactics—creating disorder by shooting the enemy officers. Both officers commanding the flank units were shot down, Lieutenant Heppe mortally. The flank units crumbled and fell back. Ensign Freyenhagen left the center and helped rally the recruits, but the American riflemen lapped around the jägers' flanks, placing the jägers in an untenable position.[44]

In the center, Captain Wrede and his experienced men took cover and, with their rifles, slowed the advance of the Continentals. Wrede may have thought about ordering the jägers to draw their swords and charge the Americans. At Iron Hill, Delaware, after hours of skirmishing, Wrede had ordered his men to draw their swords and charge, successfully pushing American riflemen from the hill. If he had such a thought, he must have immediately abandoned it, as his recruits had neither the training nor

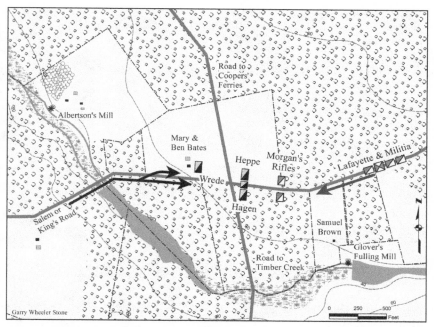

Map 12. Lafayette's detachment collides with advancing jägers.

the *esprit de corps*. And a sword charge quickly became impossible as bayonet-equipped militia came down King's Road at the quick step.[45]

South Jersey men—from Gloucester, Cumberland, and Salem Counties—charged the jägers "in fine spirits," firing, loading, advancing with leveled bayonets, and then firing again. In a November 30 letter to Frederick, ruler of Hesse, Lieutenant General Knyphausen explained that Wrede "was obliged to beat a retreat with the Jägers because the enemy charged into their ranks with the bayonet." Wrede had no choice but to fall back on his reserve unit and begin retreating as Ensign Freyenhagen struggled to reorganize the flank units. With more-experienced men, Wrede could have made a stand on the hill across from the King's Run and Albertson's millpond, but with only thirty veterans, a stand proved impossible.[46]

Map 13. Michel Capitaine du Chesnoy, *Carte de l'action de Gloucester*, detail. Burrough's and Harrison's fields are in the center immediately east of the triangular road intersection and below "i." Capitaine drew the map from officers' field notes and memories. The map's most obvious errors are the omission of the King's Run and failing to connect the Newton Creek bridge (d) with Gloucester Town. Capitaine may never have been in Gloucester County, and Lafayette may never have been in the courthouse hamlet. Map Legend (abbreviated): a. 5,000 Enemy Troops; b. Enemy baggage and troops going to Philadelphia; c. Enemy post opposite Sand Point; d. Broken bridge; e. Hessian advanced post; f. American riflemen; g. Militia that supported them; h. Parties sent into the woods; i. Place to which Hessians were chased and then held firm being supported by English troops; k. Light dragoons sent on the enemy flanks; l. Where nightfall ended fighting. (*Cornell University Library*)

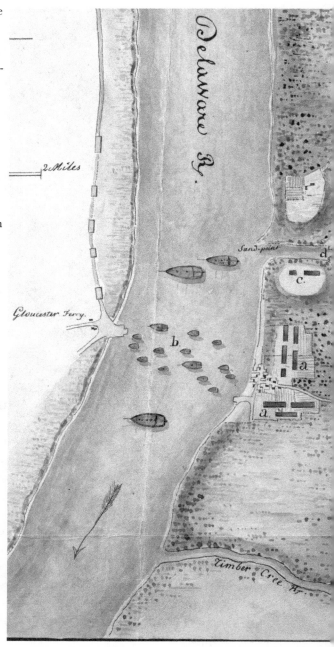

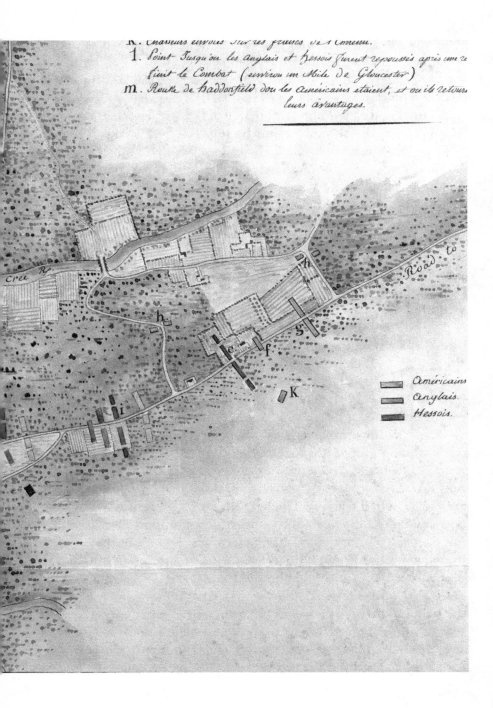

While the jägers had to beat a hasty retreat, they still presented a danger, and the experienced jägers knew how to recognize enemy officers. Cumberland County carpenter David Mulford, who had just launched one of the initial bayonet charges, turned to his men and called out, "Come well lads . . . when a ball struck him between the shoulders and he fell." Helped back to their quarters in Haddonfield, he died about seven that night. One of Mulford's privates, Thomas Harris, had his arm broken by a rifle or musket ball. Farther west along King's Road, Galloway Township's Lieutenant John Lucas died instantly when a rifle ball struck him on the left side of his chest just below the nipple. Ensign John Tilton took over command of the Galloway men until a lead ball smashed his left shoulder, a wound from which he never completely recovered. At the rear in Lieutenant Colonel Middagh's reserves, Somerset private John Auten "saw several wounded men pass by towards Haddonfield."[47]

West of the King's Run, woods lined the road, sometimes on one side, sometimes on both. In 1833, former Egg Harbor Township sergeant Richard Sayres remembered "most of the militiamen fired from behind trees, and while they continued in the woods had the advantage of the enemy & compelled them to withdraw."[48]

Wrede's military experience can be credited for keeping his detachment more or less together as they fled west on the King's Road. They had to leave their wounded behind, but Wrede had only two men captured. Then, a company of British light infantry arrived to help the jägers. The light infantry's glittering bayonets and rapid musketry made the Continentals cautious. They stayed out of reach of a bayonet charge and under cover, but they continued sniping, although the veteran British light infantry made poor targets. They, too, knew how to take cover. Based on the Capitaine map and eighteenth-century property lines, we believe that the light infantry took cover behind the fence dividing the Harrison and Burrough plantations and the fences around Ephraim and Elizabeth Albertson's farmstead. The light infantry, however, had come to extricate the jägers and not to battle Lafayette, and

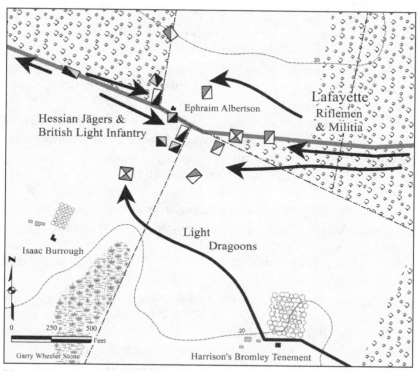

Map 14. The British light infantry marches up and skirmishing intensifies. Conjectural interpretation of the clash around the Ephraim Albertson house and the Burrough–Harrison boundary fence.

the retreat continued. If they were home, Elizabeth Albertson and her child must have been terrified as fighting raged around their dwelling—her husband then serving in the militia.[49]

While the open fields gave the light infantry and jägers clear fields of fire, they also left their south flank exposed. Michel Capitaine's map of the battle confirms the obvious: when the action arrived at the fields of militia Captain William Harrison and Isaac Burrough, the Continental light horsemen rode through the fields to outflank the enemy. If Colonel Armand carried Lafayette's orders to the light dragoons, he probably stayed to join their charge. (Armand gained a reputation as a bold, partisan officer.) Did others from Lafayette's party accompany Armand? The horses of Armand, the chevalier du Plessis, and Major Brice all suffered wounds.[50]

As soon as the light infantry and jägers resumed withdrawing, Lafayette's small force surged forward. When the fighting approached the road to the courthouse, a second British light infantry company joined, bringing with it the artillery company and the two 6-pounders formerly stationed at the jägers' picket. The Continentals, however, continued pushing until it became dangerously dark. The skirmish had begun about 4:00 PM and sunset occurred at 4:41. With the light fast disappearing, Lafayette broke off from the engagement and began a slow march back to Haddonfield. As the "enemy knowing perhaps by our drums that we were not so near came again to fire at us—but the brave Major Moriss with a part of his riflemen sent them back and pushed them very fast."[51]

The skirmish had cost the Continentals only a few casualties: two fatalities and five wounded.[52] The jägers had not been as fortunate. After darkness fell, the jägers made the long trek—almost two and a half miles—to where the fighting had begun. In his diary, Ensign Freyenhagen explained this was "in order to collect and rescue our wounded as they had been left behind before. When all were found and brought in to the nearest house, we returned to camp at 7:45 p.m. Lt Heppe died of his wounds at 9 p.m." In forty-five minutes, the jägers had suffered an officer killed, two wounded, eight rank-and-file killed, and nineteen severely wounded. Two others were missing and assumed captured.[53] No British light infantryman suffered serious wounds; their muster rolls only listed wounds preventing active service.[54]

BACK IN HADDONFIELD, the young marquis was elated with his adventure. The next day, he wrote a long letter to Washington wanting "to acquaint your excellency of a little event of last evening which tho' not very considerable in itself will certainly please you on the account of the bravery and alacrity a small party of ours

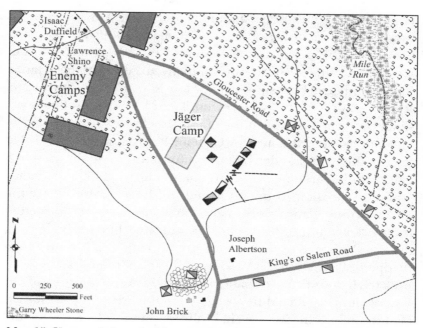

Map 15. Jägers reinforced with more light infantry and two 6-pounders. Cannonaded with case shot, the Continentals became cautious. Daylight was disappearing, so Lafayette pulled back and began marching for Haddonfield. When some of the jägers followed Lafayette's detachment, Major Morris, with some of the riflemen, pushed them back a second time.

showed in that occasion." After describing the skirmish, Lafayette returned to praising the militia and riflemen: "Such is the account of our little entertainement, which is indeed much too long for the matter, but I take the greatest pleasure to let you know that the conduct of our soldiers is above all praises. I never saw men so merry, so spirited, so desirous to go on to the enemy."[55]

At the militia quarters, their losses somewhat dampened the pride in what the men had accomplished. Late that night, Azariah More, first lieutenant of Captain Barker's Cumberland detachment, sat down to write home from Haddonfield. "We have had an engagement with a party of the enemy this evening near Little Timber Creek," he told his brother, "in which we have lost Lieutenant Mulford, as brave a man as ever lived. He was mortally wounded just as the action began, which was about 4 o'clock, was brought to this place, and died about 7 o'clock, at our quarters. We have no other loss in our company, except Thomas Harris, who had his arm broken. What our loss is in general is uncertain. It was night when we left the ground, but I am certain that it was small compared with what the enemy has lost."[56]

That evening, the men of Captain Payne's unit realized that their acting commander had not returned. The night was pitch black, and searching for Lieutenant Lucas while the enemy searched for their wounded would not be advisable. Early the next morning, James Murphy and Patrick McCollum returned to the battleground to find him. They located Lucas's body in "a ditch and covered over with some rubbish and [. . .] pretty much stripped of his clothes." Murphy and McCollum took the body back to Haddonfield. Probably, burial of Lucas, Mulford, and any other Continental fatalities occurred in the Friends' graveyard at Haddonfield.[57] In Greenwich, Mulford's family erected a memorial stone (gallery, fig. 12).

South Jersey did not forget its dead and disabled. While federal pensions did not become available until 1818, and few militiamen qualified until 1832, the state made its compensation available immediately. Hugh Jones, of the Newton Township militia, had been shot in the left side on November 25, the wound "nearly cost him his life." The rifle ball could not be extracted, and by 1795, the damage limited his ability to work. Surgeon Thomas Boulter, Captain John Stokes, Colonel—now Major General—Ellis, the county court, and a legislative committee all supported his application for future half pay. Militia officers and county courts supported similar applications. Lieutenant David Mulford's wife died in 1779, and the next year—upon receiving a certificate from the Cumberland County Court—the New Jersey Assembly voted his seven-year-old son, Enoch, a lieutenant's half pay from November 25, 1777, until he reached age eight. Levi Albertson of Gloucestertown Township, a matross in Captain Samuel Hugg's artillery company, died at Princeton in April 1776.

In 1794, his widow received a lump-sum, retroactive pension payment of 262 pounds, 10 shillings. In 1797, Captain Benjamin Whitall of Woodbury, James and Ann Whitall's son, testified that Joseph Githens had been killed during the retreat from Long Island in September 1776, and his widow subsequently received a warrant for half pay. South Jerseyans, both Whigs and Quakers, supported the war's victims.[58]

Fifty-five years later, when large numbers of Jerseymen began submitting pension claims, they had to recite the names of the officers they had served under. Only two—Richard Tice of Gloucester County and Nehemiah Dean of Middlesex County—remembered that the marquis de Lafayette was their commander. Berung VanDoren, of Somerset County, remembered he "was under the command of a French Genl; can't recollect his name."[59] What they did remember was that two of their officers—men they had elected—had been killed. Even John Auten of Somerset County remembered seeing mortally wounded "Lieutenant Mulford." While Lafayette's success on King's Road proved important for the American Revolution, South Jersey neighborhoods remembered the losses.[60]

CORNWALLIS ESCAPES

On November 26, the morning after the skirmish, Major General Greene rode into Haddonfield.[61] What the generals learned from Weedon, Lafayette, and others proved disappointing. Greene wrote Washington at 4:00 PM:

> I am sorry our march will prove a fruitless one. The enemy have drawn themselves down upon the Peninsula of Gloucester: the ships are drawn up to cover the troops. There is but one road that leads down to the point, on each side the ground is swampy and full of thick underbrush that it makes the approaches impracticable almost. [. . .] I proposed to the Gentlemen drawing up in front of the enemy and to attack their Picquet and endeavour to draw them out but they were all against it, from the improbability of the enemies coming out. The Marquis with about 400 militia and the rifle Corps at-

tacked the enemies Picquet last evening, kill'd about 20 and wounded many more and took about 20 prisoners. The marquis is charmed with the spirited behaviour of the militia and Rifle Corps.[62]

Another part of Greene's letter included a response to Washington's letter of eight o'clock the previous night—a letter Greene received only after reaching Haddonfield. Washington expressed concern that with Cornwallis returning to Philadelphia and with two and a half divisions of the Continental army in New Jersey, General Howe would attack the Continental army encampment at Whitemarsh. (Howe did, nine days later.) Therefore, Washington ordered the Continental troops back to Pennsylvania.

Greene immediately sent orders to Glover's, Muhlenberg's, and Weedon's brigades—they had not yet reached Haddonfield—to halt and march back toward the Burlington-Bristol ferry. They reached Mount Holly in the evening. Lafayette also left Haddonfield on the twenty-sixth and arrived back in Whitemarsh on the twenty-eighth. Huntington's and Varnum's brigades spent the night in Haddonfield. That evening, the twenty-sixth, British sailors burned a Gloucester Town tenement belonging to the local militia commander, Captain William Harrison, "for the part he took against them."[63]

The next morning at five o'clock, Huntington's brigade marched for Mount Holly. Greene was bitterly disappointed that he had not "met" Lord Cornwallis. So he sent Lieutenant Colonel Jeremiah Olney, 2nd Rhode Island, with part of Varnum's brigade west on King's Road to attack the jäger picket. Greene would be disappointed again. Nearing the jägers, Olney found that Captain Wrede had pulled his men back so close to the main encampment that an attack would not be practical. Olney returned to Haddonfield, and the brigade marched for Mount Holly. Greene wrote orders for the militia to annoy Cornwallis and to limit future foraging by driving cattle back from the river and creek banks and taking up the decking of bridges along the Delaware. Greene left the riflemen and Captain Lee's troop of light horse to encourage

the militia and contain the enemy. That evening, Greene returned to Mount Holly.[64]

Sending all the troops back across the Delaware took more
time than Greene had hoped. The shortage of scows prevented
the efficient ferrying of the wagons and artillery, and Muhlenberg's division was delayed at Mount Holly in a search for food,
but all of Greene's detachment arrived at Whitemarsh before
Howe attacked on December 5, 1777.[65]

FINAL SHOTS

At Gloucester Town, during the morning of the twenty-seventh,
schooners and sloops transported Cornwallis's remaining ani-
mals, baggage, and artillery across the river, a process that
Colonel Richard Butler, with the riflemen and some militia,
watched from the woods. Captain Henry Lee and his troop of
light dragoons accompanied Butler to protect his flanks should
he have to retreat. At noon, British seamen began loading the infantry onto flatboats. The 1st Battalion of British Light Infantry
departed last. About 2:00 PM, as the flatboats left the beach, two
hundred or so rebels appeared at the edge of the adjacent woods
and opened fire, wounding an officer, several soldiers, and a sea-
man.[66] Jäger Freyenhagen was impressed: "The Rebels followed
us to the water where they had to withstand musket fire from the
boats and a strong cannonade from H.M.S. *Vigilant* plus a frigate
[sloop-of-war *Zebra*] and a row-galley [*Cornwallis*]." The insur-
gents' courage was apparent to the British and German troops already landed on the far shore.[67]

The *Vigilant* battery ship was anchored near the ferry wharf.
Once the flatboats no longer blocked their lines of fire, its gun
crews opened fire with their 24-pounders. Butler wisely pulled
back the riflemen and militia.[68]

By evening, Cornwallis's troops had returned to their barracks
in Philadelphia, and the Continentals had lost control of the
Delaware River. However, Lafayette's skirmish on Haddonfield-
Gloucester Road would have enduring political significance.

———————

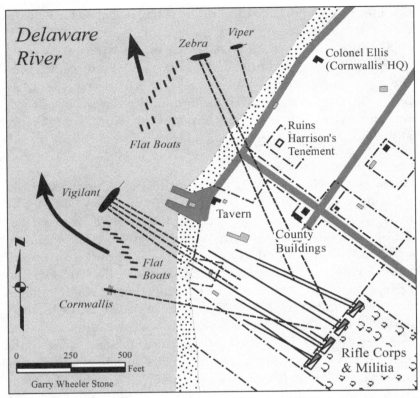

Map 16. Final shots, November 27, 1777. As the last British infantry boarded flatboats, Continental riflemen advanced to the edge of the woods and began firing. Some riflemen or militia may have infiltrated the hamlet. One shot from the British cannonade struck Colonel Ellis's home. The *Vigilant* was anchored near Hugg's wharf. We have no information on the location of the other vessels covering the embarkation.

ON NOVEMBER 28, the residents of Gloucester Town probably gave no thought to the future significance of Lafayette's adventure. They had endured burnt fences, pastures and fields of wheat and rye grazed to the ground, mows emptied of hay, chickens and pigs eaten, and cattle and horses transported to Philadelphia. Soldiers had emptied pantries and cellars of food and drink, and lightweight portable items, especially residents' clothing and linens, had disappeared into knapsacks. Across from Hugg's tavern stood the charred ruins of the Harrisons' Malt House tenement, while south of the Little Timber Creek bridge, the ruins of the plantations of two rebel commissaries still smoldered.[69]

Along King's Road, where the fighting had transpired, less damage had occurred. Fences had been pushed over, but John Brick, Isaac Burrough, Charles Saxton, and Ephraim Albertson (or their servants) easily restacked the rails. Other grimmer reminders of the fighting remained: splotches of dried blood and, along the edges of the road, the graves of jägers Friedrich Schoinanus, Niclaus Koch, Caspar Weyrauch, and Adam Schelhasse. (Three wounded jägers would die before the end of November.) Lieutenant Heppe's men would have carried his body back to their camp so he could be given a proper military burial, but where did they dig his grave? Gloucester Town had no church, no community graveyard. In the 1840s, residents pointed out a slight elevation in one of John Brick's fields as the burial place of battle casualties.[70]

NEWS OF THE BATTLE SPREADS . . . AND CHANGES

In Philadelphia, well-connected officers of the garrison quickly learned about the action along King's Road. In their journals, Major John André and engineer John Montrésor matter-of-factly note the skirmishes of November 25 and 27 and the jäger casualties. The losses were not notable: it was a bloody war with almost daily losses as the light troops of both sides probed each other.[71] Across the Delaware from Gloucester Town, the residents of Chester County only knew that sustained gunfire occurred in Gloucestertown Township. When an express rider from the Continental camp at Whitemarsh reached the Continental Congress at York, Pennsylvania, on the twenty-eighth, he told delegates of heavy firing in New Jersey. The following day, Rhode Island delegate William Ellery relayed a report to Nicolas Cooke of "a battle between Genl Green & Cornwallis." While almost immediately, Washington's letter to President Laurens provided information on Lafayette's "little event," a letter to a delegate from Major John Clark—one of Washington's chief intelligence agents—kept the rumor of an additional battle alive. And the rumor mill was in overdrive. On December 2, New York delegate James Duane wrote New York Governor George Clinton "a Report prevails that [. . .] Cornwallis is taken Prisoner & his Division broken." The following day, President Henry Laurens wrote John Adams "that from different & corroborating accounts Lord Cornwallis was killed or wounded, that [. . .] the Enemy was beat, left 30 dead on the field & crossed the Water after having set fire to that pretty little Town by which the whole was consumed." It was all rumor, with a healthy dose of wishful thinking. Washington never believed it, and on November 28, the commander in chief learned that Cornwallis had safely returned to Philadelphia.[72]

A THOUGHTFUL OBSERVER of Lafayette on November 24–25, 1777, would have found that the marquis's actions confirmed earlier impressions: the young man exuded ambition, bravery, and charisma, and believed in hard work. He realistically claimed no great victory in his report to Washington. He was thoughtful and generous, sharing credit for the victory by complimenting the riflemen and the militia, and in his report to Washington, naming all their commanding officers—even the lieutenant commanding the ten light dragoons. Back at Whitemarsh, he again praised the performance of the riflemen to Washington, and the next day or so, Lafayette wrote Colonel Butler that Washington "desires his thanks should be made to the Officers and soldiers of the brave detachment of riflemen under your's and major moriss' command." The marquis's conduct before and after the skirmish confirmed Major General Greene's November 21 opinion that Lafayette was "a most sweet temperd young gentleman."[73]

But was the "young gentleman" ready to take on the responsibilities of a major general? On King's Road, Lafayette showed he had many of the attributes of a successful battalion commander but no more. The skirmish was a limited action between battalion-sized forces along a single road. Less than four hours elapsed between the time Lafayette led the militia out of Haddonfield and the time they returned. How much of the marquis's success could be attributed to the help that he received from Colonels Armand, Butler, and Ellis? How much of the Continentals' success stemmed from Cornwallis's focus on getting his troops and forage to Philadelphia, rather than tangling with unknown forces in the broken ground east of Gloucester Town? Only in the future—after Barren Hill, Monmouth, and Rhode Island—can we judge whether in 1777–1778 the young man had the temperament and skills required of a major general commanding a division.

Already, however, he exhibited a hint of a trait that would appear throughout the American Revolution. Lafayette needed the emotional support of Washington, his surrogate father, and the friendship of Alexander Hamilton, John Laurens (son of President Henry Laurens), and the others of Washington's military family. The marquis disliked being away from the center of power. He did not stay in Haddonfield to continue reconnoitering and harassing the enemy troops at Gloucester Town. On November 26, Lafayette and his aides rode for Whitemarsh.[74]

FIVE

The Promotion of Major General the Marquis de Lafayette

SHORTLY AFTER THE MARQUIS'S ARRIVAL in late July 1777, Washington became concerned about the gap between Lafayette's commission from the Continental Congress and Lafayette's understanding of his commission. Lafayette received a commission as a major general on July 31 "because of his zeal, illustrious family and connexions," but it was widely understood that the commission was honorific and "without pay or command." The written commission, however, failed to so state the lack of a command, and the young man wanted one. In August, Washington wrote Delegate Benjamin Harrison for clarification, and Harrison wrote back that Lafayette's commission "was merely Honorary."[1] On October 14, from the hospital at Bethlehem, Pennsylvania, Lafayette, who had suffered a leg wound at Brandywine, wrote Washington "with the confidence of a son, of a friend" that he "would deserve the reproaches of my friends and family if I would leave the advantages of mine to stay in a country where I could not find the occasions of distinguishing myself." [2] On November 1, the same day Henry Laurens began serving as president of the Continental Congress, Washington wrote him:

> I feel myself in a delicate situation with respect to the Marquis Le Fayette. He is extremely solicitous of having a Command equal to his rank, & professes very different ideas as to the purposes of his appointment from those Congress have mentioned to me. [. . .] It appears to me, from a consideration of his illustrious and important connections—the attachment which he has manifested to our cause, and the consequences, which his return in disgust might produce, that it will be adviseable to gratify him in his wishes. [3]

Again, Washington did not obtain the response that he and Lafayette desired. During the evening of November 26, Washington received two letters that encouraged him to ask again. The first, from the elated marquis, contained a long description of the skirmish, admitting that it was a "very trifling" affair but that it would please Washington "on the account of bravery and alacrity" of the Continental soldiers. The second letter was from Major General Greene. To an overall description of the discouraging military situation, Greene included an account of the King's Road skirmish favorable to Lafayette, noting, "The Marquis is determined to be in the way of danger." That evening, Washington included in a letter to Laurens a recommendation that Lafayette be given command of a Continental army division. [4]

The dispatch rider from Haddonfield appears to have arrived while Washington was dictating the letter to Laurens. In it, Washington had already addressed frontier defense, international affairs, and the reenlistment of Virginia soldiers when he requested the delegates' "determination respecting the Marquis de la Fayette. He is more & More solicitous to be in actual service." Worried that his protégé might return to France "in disgust," involving "some unfavorable consequences," Washington noted that the Continental army was short of division commanders, and that he, Washington, was convinced that Lafayette "possesses a large share of that Military ardor which generally characterises the Nobility of his Country." To illustrate, Washington added Greene's description of the skirmish to the end of the paragraph.[5]

Washington's letter reached Laurens at York on Saturday, November 29. Agreeing that Lafayette should be given a command, Laurens shared the letter with the delegates, among whom it had the desired effect. Massachusetts Delegate James Lovell wrote John Adams "Fayette being with Genl. Greene in the Jersies fell upon a Pickett of the Enemy, killed 20, took 20 & wounded many. [. . .] Genl. Greene says the Marquis seems determined to court Danger. I wish more were so determined." In a similar vein, New York's William Duer wrote that Lafayette "attack'd a Picquet of the Enemy in Jersey. . . . It is said he behaved with great Intrepedity; and I beleive with some Experience will make a good officer." On November 30, Henry Laurens wrote his son John that he had shared the letter with several members of Congress and they "expressed their wishes that the Marquis may be appointed to the Command of a division." Laurens was confident that when Washington's letter was read to Congress on Monday, they would agree.[6]

Laurens was correct. On Monday, December 1, 1777, Congress resolved "it is highly agreeable to Congress that the Marquis de la Fayette be appointed to the command of a division in the continental army." Moreover, the delegates honored Lafayette by ordering an extract from Washington's letter published. The extract began "THE Marquis de la Fayette went to Jersey with General Green, and I find he has not been inactive there" and reproduced Greene's account of the skirmish. The extract was published in Baltimore on December 9 and reproduced in Philadelphia, Annapolis, Williamsburg, and elsewhere.[7] The merits of the brave young Frenchman were spreading beyond the Continental army.

In his general orders for December 4, 1777, Washington wrote, "Major General The Marquis La Fayette is to take the command of the division lately commanded by General Stephen." Washington's success in gaining a command for Lafayette solved two problems: it kept his protégé happy, and it filled a vacancy. After a lengthy court-martial, on November 20, Major General Adam Stephen had been dismissed from the army. Stephen's problems included chronic intoxication and a lack of loyalty to the commander in chief. To a degree, Stephen's court-martial paralleled the 1778 court-martial of Major General Charles Lee, with Washington loyalists exaggerating the deficiencies of Washington's critics.[8]

Washington was aware of Adam Stephen's strengths and weaknesses. They had served together in the French and Indian War and later competed for the same seat in the Virginia House of Burgesses. In 1775, Stephen received an appointment as colonel of the 4th Virginia Regiment. There he continued to extend his reputation as a hardworking and versatile officer; then he was promoted. On September 6, 1776, the Continental Congress made him a brigadier, and the following February, it elevated him to major general. Stephen's promotions, especially the second, may have led to his downfall. He had never been a good administrator, and now, two removes from the regiments, his job had become mostly administrative. Moreover, he now served at a level where he could offer annoying advice to the commander in chief. And why not? Stephen was older than Washington, better educated, and had more military experience. Worse, he now felt free to share his doubts about Washington's abilities with Washington's critics in the Congress. Annoying as Washington may have found Stephen's friends and criticisms, Stephen would have kept command of his division except for his abuse of alcohol.[9]

In July 1777, on a march from Chester, New York, to Philadelphia, Stephen gave confused and sometimes contradictory orders—and evidently, the confusion derived in part from a bottle. After arriving at a Delaware River ferry, Stephen was observed "in open view of all the soldiers very drunk taking snuff out of the Boxes of strumpets." This was hardly the behavior of an officer and a gentleman. Then, on September 11, at the Battle of Brandywine, his division performed well, although Stephen may have been drinking. The Battle of Germantown proved to be his downfall. During the retreat, Stephen was so drunk he was unable to assist his brigadiers.[10]

Stephen's performance at Germantown unleashed a torrent of complaints from his officers. Stephen tried to clear his name by asking for a court of inquiry, but the court found grounds for a court-martial. Following a trial that lasted from November 3 to 20, 1777, the court's members found that he was "guilty of unofficer-like behavior, in the retreat from Germantown, owing to inattention, or want of judgement; and that he has been frequently intoxicated since in the service, to the prejudice of good order and military discipline," and they dismissed Stephen from the army. He appealed the decision to the Continental Congress, but the delegates knew of Stephen's problems and took no action.[11]

The charges against Stephen had spread far. Lafayette, in the hospital in Pennsylvania, had heard of them. On October 14, he wrote Washington that if Stephen resigned, his "division of virginians . . . would be the most agreable for me." On December 4, 1777, he got his wish.[12]

LAFAYETTE TAKES COMMAND

Now the young man was responsible for nine regiments forming the two brigades of Generals Woodford and Scott. Nominally, these two brigades totaled 3,436 officers and men, but of them— at the beginning of December—only 1,957 (57 percent) were "present fit for duty and on duty." The others were "sick present," "sick absent," on command, on furlough, or lacking clothing. At the end of the month, of a total of 326 officers and men in Daniel Morgan's 11th Virginia Regiment, only eighty-one were on duty with the regiment. Of those not on duty, sixty-six were sick, seventy-eight were on command, twelve were on furlough, and eighty-nine were incapacitated for "wanting shoes, etc." Of the seventy-eight "on command," probably most served with Colonel Morgan in the Rifle Corps. There, Captain Gabriel Long, 11th Virginia, commanded the largest company.[13]

On December 4, 1777, the marquis had little time to worry about how many men he had and did not have. That evening, General Howe led about ten thousand men from Philadelphia to attack the Continental camp at Whitemarsh. Over the following three days, as the British army clashed with the Continentals' forward line on Edge Hill, Lafayette's two brigades were in the second line behind the abatis.[14] While Lafayette circulated among his troops, he began a charm offensive to raise morale. As he later wrote Henry Laurens, "Honor will raise from praises. . . . I intend for this purpose to pay to the lieutenants of my division the same politeness and regard which is payed here to General officers."[15]

Circulating among his troops, Lafayette discovered that they were miserably clothed. In the same December 13 letter to Laurens in which he had written about morale, he wrote passionately about the "quite nacked fellows incapable of service for want of cloathes, shoes &c. I have many in my division." A lack of necessities prevented men from doing their duty and led to sickness and desertion. Lack of clothing and shoes loomed large in Washington's mind, even ordering men to press (confiscate) clothing. On December 27, encouraged by the arrival of cloth in Virginia and Boston, Washington and several generals discussed how to have it made up into uniforms. The next day, Lafayette followed up with lengthy, detailed recommendations on every aspect of winter and summer uniforms, soldiers' hygiene, and how officers should inspect them.[16] Lafayette always would be a soldier's general, keenly aware of his troops' need to be adequately fed, clothed, and paid.

While a general held onerous responsibilities, as Lafayette led his troops from Whitemarsh toward Valley Forge, he commanded as a happy young man, a real—not honorary—major general. Still, he was realistic. On December 16, in a letter to his father-in-law from Gulph Mills, Pennsylvania, the marquis wrote "this work will be very useful for my development. [. . .] I read, I study, I examine, I listen, I think, and out of all of that I try to form an opinion into which I cram as much common sense as possible."[17]

LAFAYETTE RECEIVES A SWORD, AND THE SKIRMISH BECOMES A BATTLE
If any of the youngsters who fought along King's Road on November 25 thought they had been in a battle, the veterans among the militia quickly disillusioned them. It had been only a skirmish, and despite the passage of time, it remained a skirmish fifty-five

years later, when survivors submitted pension declarations. They described it as a "skirmish," "pretty smart skirmish," "severe skirmish," or "pretty smart engagement." Only the confused declaration of Samuel Bowen listed it as a battle.[18] No riflemen appear to have suffered an injury worth remembering. For most of the participants from the Rifle Corps, the action quickly escaped their memories, sandwiched as it was between the Battles of Saratoga and Whitemarsh. Only two members of Morgan's corps submitted pension applications mentioning service at Haddonfield.[19] For Lafayette, however, the November 1777 skirmish in Gloucester County loomed large. It represented the first time the young man had led troops in combat.

At Valley Forge, the news of the French alliance with the United States arrived April 30, 1778. Lafayette immediately began thinking of returning home to rejoin the French army and fight the English in Europe. However, Louis XVI sent no request for Lafayette to return, and he knew that the French army and navy would need time to prepare before launching an attack on Great Britain. Moreover, Lafayette remained busy throughout the late spring with preparations for the summer, followed by the Barren Hill reconnaissance, the Monmouth Campaign, and the failed attempt to drive the English out of Newport, Rhode Island. Not until mid-September do Lafayette's letters reflect a renewed desire to return to France. On September 13, he wrote his wife, "I can also hope that this hardship will end soon and that the moment when we shall meet again (dear heart), can no longer be far off." Two weeks later, the marquis wrote Washington that he wished to be granted leave from his New England duties and would "ride as an express in changing horses on the Road" to rejoin Washington. Lafayette wanted to discuss his future with Washington before the French fleet left Boston.[20]

Washington granted Lafayette's request to take leave. The two men spent a day together at Fishkill, New York, then the marquis hurried on to Philadelphia. With him he carried a letter in which Washington approved his application to Congress for a leave of absence. In it, Washington set the tone for the marquis's leave taking, citing "the generous motives which first induced him to cross the Atlantic. [. . .] Reasons equally laudable now engage his return to France." Washington concluded, "I shall always be happy to give such a testimony of his services, as his bravery and conduct, on all occasions, entitle him to, and I have no doubt that Congress will add suitable expressions of their sense of his merit."[21]

The delegates to Congress understood that Lafayette's return to France created an opportunity to gain more support for the Revolution. They provided him with a beautifully composed recommendation to "Great faithful and beloved Friend and Ally" Louis XVI and voted to present the marquis an elegant sword advertising his American service. Conrad-Alexandre Gérard, the French minister to the United States, wrote his own glowing recommendation, but there was more. As Lafayette traveled to France, he could carry new instructions to Benjamin Franklin, Congress's senior representative at the court of Versailles. These had to be composed, as well as new plans for an invasion of Canada. Lafayette had hoped to stay only three days in Philadelphia and then rush back to Boston to board a French frigate, but the days stretched into weeks. Lafayette did not leave Philadelphia until October 28, and he became ill on his trip back to Boston. On November 4, the French fleet sailed without him. A frustrated marquis was forced to wait in America until departing for France on the *Alliance* frigate January 12, 1779. With him he carried a glowing letter of recommendation from Washington to Franklin. In it, among other accomplishments, Washington cited Lafayette's "success in Jersey before he had recovered of his Wound, in an affair where he commanded Militia against British Grenadiers [jägers]." Despite terrible weather and an attempted mutiny, the *Alliance* made a fast voyage, reaching Brest in only twenty-one days. Lafayette entered Paris by February 13.[22]

William Carmichael, the marquis's friend, penned one of the letters Lafayette carried. On October 30, 1778, Carmichael, now one of the Maryland delegates to the Continental Congress, wrote Benjamin Franklin on how to further the American cause through Lafayette's return. Carmichael was particularly qualified to do this. He had worked with Franklin while serving as secretary to the other American agent, Silas Deane, and in February 1777, Carmichael had served as the conduit by which Lafayette communicated with the American agents. Carmichael suggested that Franklin rush Congress's resolves and letter of recommendation to Versailles before Lafayette appeared there. "I am sure all the consequence he can derive from the influence of his Family or from his own merit will be exerted for our Interests."[23]

Congress had voted Lafayette a commemorative sword, and in the last paragraph of his letter, Carmichael advised Franklin that Lafayette wished to have his Paris cutler produce the sword. Lafayette's aide-de-camp, Michel Capitaine, added an approximation of the cutler's name and address: "*Leger Fourbissier Derriere L'Opera à Paris.*" As the sword would serve to highlight Lafayette's American career, Carmichael suggested "allusions to the scenes of actions in which he most distinguished Himself": Brandywine, Barren Hill, Monmouth, Rhode Island, and "Glocester where he drove Ld. Cornwallis."[24]

Lafayette's sword cutler was Claude-Raymond Liger (1720–1802), *fourbisseur* (sword-maker)[25] to the duc de Chartres and the comte de Clarmont. His establishment stood near the Royal Opera at the corner of Coquillière Street and the Alley of the Old Augustines. In 1785–1786, Liger fabricated ten more swords for Congress.[26]

Benjamin Franklin appears to have been largely responsible for the design of the sword. While he and Lafayette met occasionally from March to May 1779, the marquis had many distractions. He had rejoined the French army as colonel of the King's Dragoon Regiment, and he was intensely involved in projected raids on English ports, plans that evolved into preparations for a French invasion of England. During the summer, while the sword was under production in Paris, Lafayette was at French ports with troops poised to cross the English Channel. When, at Le Havre, he first saw the finished product, he expressed surprise at the "flattering attributes" incorporated in the "Noble present." While

Lafayette and Franklin may have discussed which events to commemorate on the leaves of the guard, Franklin and Liger were responsible for the details.[27]

The sword's production began with ideas, ideas then converted into artist's sketches, sketches that once approved became full-scale renderings—renderings that survive in our National Archives. Then the artisans took over: the cutler who forged the blade and the steel foundations of the hilt, the goldsmith who decorated the guard, grip, pommel, and bow, and the engraver who cut the designer's drawings into scenes on the guard. The sword was a major commission: It cost 4,800 French livres, the equivalent of 200 British guineas (£210), or the modern (2020) equivalent of some £37,361 or $51,232. The sword was not completed until August.[28]

Claude-Raymond Liger or his son delivered the completed sword August 24, 1779, and Franklin sat down to compose an elegant cover letter to Lafayette that opens, "Sir, The Congress sensible of your Merit towards the United States, but unable adequately to reward it, determined to present you with a Sword, as a small Mark of their grateful Acknowledgement." Franklin sent the sword to Le Havre with his secretary—his nineteen-year-old grandson, William Temple Franklin (Temple). Temple Franklin's departure may have been delayed. As word of the sword's completion spread, at least one request arrived to see it—from Madame Brillon, one of Franklin's admirers.[29]

Lafayette was pleased with the sword but did not respond immediately. The twenty-one-year-old colonel of dragoons was having too good a time expounding on the planned invasion of England to an enthusiastic listener. On August 29, as Temple Franklin prepared to return to Passy, Lafayette composed two messages to Benjamin Franklin. The first was a short, carefully composed letter for public consumption. In it, the marquis thanked the United States for its past favors and the noble present, noting that the military scenes would remind him of "American Bravery and patriotic Spirit." Lafayette penned the second letter personally to Franklin. It began with thanks after which

Lafayette posed a question for Franklin: could his grandson accompany Lafayette as an aide-de-camp on the English expedition? Both Franklin and the comte de Vergennes assented, but the expedition never took place as the French and Spanish fleets failed to neutralize the British navy.[30]

Lafayette cherished the sword for the remainder of his life. During his imprisonment in Prussia and Austria (1792–1797,) his wife buried it for safekeeping, which destroyed the steel blade but preserved its gold guard and hilt. The sword was restored with a blade taken from another, and at Lafayette's death it was on display in the library of his home, the Château de la Grange-Bléneau. In 1835, Dr. Jules Germain Cloquet, a noted surgeon and medical illustrator, visited the chateau and drew the sword for use in his two-volume work, *Recollections of the Private Life of General Lafayette*. Engraved, his drawings illustrate the first chapter of volume 2. Besides two elevations of the sword, Cloquet drew each of the battle scenes, and his drawings show that on the edges of the guard, each scene is named. While *Recollections* is a poor biography, Cloquet's description of La Grange and its collections are important, especially as the sword has disappeared.

The drawings show that it is Benjamin Franklin who renamed the "sharp skirmish" the "Battle of Gloucester." In the design development drawings, the scenes are unidentified. On the completed sword, they are named. Franklin's role is confirmed by an undated note from Liger to Franklin, in which Liger requests "pour la legende [inscription] wich you was to send him for the sword of the Marquis."[31] Thus the participant's skirmish, Carmichael's "action," and Michael Capitaine's "l'action de Gloucester" became the "Battle of Gloucester." "Battle" and "Action" have six letters each. In substituting "Battle" for "Action," Franklin inflated the marquis's résumé to enhance his prestige as the young man advocated for French support for the American war. Franklin was an old hand at inflating résumés, having advertised Captain Friedrich Wilhelm von Steuben as a Prussian lieutenant general.

Lafayette's "*Epéé Dor a Bataille*" (golden battle sword) met the expectations of the Continental Congress and Franklin. John Adams observed as much. Formerly a delegate from Massachusetts to the Congress, he now resided in Paris helping Franklin and Arthur Lee negotiate with Britain. On February 29, 1780, as Lafayette prepared to return to America to rejoin the Continental army, Adams wrote his friend, James Lovell, a Massachusetts delegate to the Congress:

> My dear Friend
>
> I cannot let the Marquis go off, without a Line to you. He took leave of the King a few days ago, in the Uniform of an American Major General, and attracted the Eyes of the whole Court more than ever. He had on no doubt his American Sword which is indeed a Beauty, and which he shews with great Pleasure, upon proper Occasions. The workmanship is exquisite, and there are Emblems on it, representing him, in all the most remarkable Situations he has been in in America.[32]

Of these "remarkable Situations," the most important was the "Battle of Gloucester."

Epilogue

Lafayette: The Man Becomes a Symbol

THE SKIRMISH ALONG King's Road provided the key that unlocked Lafayette's heroic future. During the next fifty-six years, he became the idol of American Whigs, an on-again, off-again favorite of Louis XVI and Marie Antoinette, commander of the Paris National Guard, and a political prisoner. He boycotted Napoleon, supported revolutions in the 1820s, and helped install a French constitutional monarch in 1830.[1]

Recall that during October and November 1777, Lafayette had hinted broadly that unless he gained command responsibilities, he would return to France. But, enabled by Washington, Major General Nathanael Greene, Brigadier General George Weedon, and Colonels Richard Butler and Joseph Ellis, the marquis won the Battle of Gloucester, and nine days later Congress granted him command of a division of the Continental army. In February 1779, he returned triumphantly to France and in August received a presentation of a golden battle sword advertising his heroic résumé. Lafayette had been very, very lucky in being rich, in finding a mentoring father figure in Commander in Chief George Washington, in not being bayonetted at Brandywine or shot on King's Road at Gloucester.

What if Lafayette had not won at Gloucester? If Captain Wrede had asked for British light infantry support when the jägers marched toward the King's Run, would there have been a rebel victory? Without a victory on King's Road, would Congress have granted Lafayette command of a Continental army division? It seems unlikely. Without the Congress's promotion during spring and summer 1778, the marquis would have remained an aide-de-camp to Washington. Only his promotion made it possible for him to command troops at Barren Hill, Monmouth, and Rhode Island. Without these command responsibilities, it is highly likely that in fall 1778, a bitterly disappointed young man would have returned to France. There he would have been received not as a national hero but as a young adventurer who had disobeyed his family and his sovereign. European history would have evolved differently, and the United States would have lost a hero—and, of more significance, perhaps a different relationship with France, whose assistance to the Revolution proved decisive.

The charming marquis remained a hero to Americans for the rest of his life and beyond. From 1779 to 1783, whether in France or serving as a division commander in the Continental army, he worked tirelessly to advance the interests of the United States. In August 1784, he returned to the United States to see his "dear general," to say goodbye to his army comrades, and to share in the glory of peace. Over four and a half months, he toured the country, welcomed as a hero everywhere.[2] Forty years later, he visited America again, this time as a guest of the government. In February 1824, pursuant to a resolution of Congress, President James Monroe—a young army major at the Battle of Monmouth in 1778—wrote Lafayette inviting him to visit the United States. Lafayette, his son George Washington Lafayette, and the marquis's secretary sailed from France July 13, 1824.[3]

Over the next thirteen months, Lafayette visited all twenty-four states, some of them twice. He enjoyed a steamboat trip on the Mississippi, endured a shipwreck on the Ohio, and visited battlefields of the Revolution and the War of 1812. Everywhere he traveled, people received him with great celebration and banquets. The tour proved to be as exciting and exhausting as a presidential campaign.[4] Lafayette spent most of August 1825, his last month in America, in Washington, DC, as a guest of President John Quincy Adams in the White House. On September 6, Adams hosted a state dinner at the White House to celebrate the marquis's sixty-eighth birthday. The next day, cabinet ministers, other dignitaries, the militias of Alexandria, Georgetown, and Washington, and a crowd of citizens stood on the bank of the Potomac to bid farewell to Lafayette. The marquis and his suite boarded the steamboat *Mount Vernon* for the trip down the Potomac to the bay. There, the USS *Brandywine* waited to carry Lafayette back to France.[5]

Lafayette died in his Paris home May 20, 1834, at seventy-six. When the news reached the United States, the country went into mourning: flags at half-staff, twenty-four-gun salutes, and black armbands.[6] It was the passing of an era: Lafayette was the last surviving leader of the American Revolution. Long before his death, localities took his name: Fayette County, Virginia (now Kentucky) in 1780, and in 1783, Fayette County, Pennsylvania, and Fayetteville, North Carolina. Now there are over one hundred places in the United States named after Lafayette including counties (17); cities, towns, and townships (77); urban places (10); plus a college, theaters, hotels, and at least ten high schools, from one of which coauthor Garry Stone graduated.[7]

Almost ninety years after his death, his memory served as a symbol of the debt the United States owed France for its assistance during the American Revolution, a debt the United States felt it was repaying when it entered World War I. On July 4, 1917, at Lafayette's grave in Paris, Lieutenant Colonel Charles E. Stanton, an aide to General John Pershing, famously concluded a speech with, "Lafayette, we are here."[8]

It was a legacy made possible in great measure by a victory on King's Road in Gloucester County, New Jersey, November 25, 1777.

Notes

Abbreviations used in notes

ASNJ	Archives of the State of New Jersey (52 vols. published in 3 series, 1880–1986)
CCHS	Camden County Historical Society
GC	Gloucester County Government
GCHS	Gloucester County Historical Society
GCityHS	Gloucester City Historical Society
HABS	Historic American Buildings Survey, Library of Congress
NA	National Archives
NDAR	*Naval Documents of the American Revolution*
NJ	New Jersey Government (Colony and State)
NJSA	New Jersey State Archives, Trenton
PA Arch	Pennsylvania Archives
Pension	Revolutionary War Pension and Bounty-Land Warrant Application Files
PMHB	*Pennsylvania Magazine of History and Biography*
RG	Record Group at the National Archives

INTRODUCTION

1. Louis Gottschalk, *Lafayette Comes to America* (Chicago: University of Chicago Press, 1935), 2-48.

2. Ibid., 49-50; *Encyclopædia Britannica*, "Broglie, de" (Cambridge University, 1911), 4:626-27; Francis Wharton, ed., *The Revolutionary Diplomatic Correspondence of the United States*, 6 vols. (Washington, DC: Government Printing Office, 1889), 2:72-74, 74n, 218, 218n; A. E. Zucker, *General de Kalb, Lafayette's Mentor* (Chapel Hill: University of North Carolina Press, 1966), 95-107.

3. Christopher Hodapp, *Solomon's Builders: Freemasons, Founding Fathers and the Secrets of Washington, D.C.* (Berkeley, CA: Ulysses Press, 2007), 12-88.

4. Zucker, *General de Kalb*, 95-98.

5. Bruce E. Mowday, *Lafayette at Brandywine: The Making of an American Hero* (Fort Lee, NJ: Barricade Books, 2021), 45; Christy L. Pichichero, *The Military Enlightenment: War and Culture in the French Empire from Louis XIV to Napoleon* (Ithaca, NY: Cornell University Press, 2017), 69.

6. Gottschalk, *Lafayette Comes*, 71-82; Zucker, *General de Kalb*, 51-84.

7. Zucker, *General de Kalb*, 44-95.

8. Gottschalk, *Lafayette Comes*, 74-76; Silas Deane, *The Deane Papers, 1774–1790*, vol. 1, Collections of the New-York Historical Society for the Year 1886 (New York: New-York Historical Society, 1887), 342-45, 359-60, 404-11; Gilbert du Motier, marquis de Lafayette, *Lafayette in the Age of the American Revolution*, ed. Stanley J. Idzerda (Ithaca, NY: Cornell University Press, 1977–), 1:17 (hereinafter Lafayette, *Papers*).

9. Gottschalk, *Lafayette Comes*, 76-80.

10. Ibid., 83-123, 134-42; Lafayette, *Papers*, 1:17-19, 50; Elizabeth S. Kite, "Lafayette and His Companions on the 'Victoire,'" *Records of the American Catholic Society* 45, no. 1 (March 1934): 1-32; Francis B. Heitman, *Historical Register of Officers of the Continental Army* (Baltimore: Genealogical Publishing, 1967), 143; Peter J. Guthorn, *American Maps and Map Makers of the Revolution* (Monmouth Beach, NJ: Philip Freneau Press, 1966), 9-12; George Washington, *The Papers of George Washington: Revolutionary War Series*, ed. Philander D. Chase et al. (Charlottesville: University Press of Virginia, 1985–), 11:5, 17:245; B. F. Stevens, *B. F. Stevens's Facsimiles of Manuscripts in European Archives Relating to America, 1773–1783*, vol. 1 (London: Malby & Sons, 1889), 29; Glenn Campbell, senior historian, Historic Annapolis, MD, provided crucial information on Brice's location from 1772–1776. He is preparing an article on the Revolutionary War service of the Brice brothers.

11. Louis Gottschalk, *Lafayette Joins the American Army* (Chicago: University of Chicago Press, 1965), 1-26; Washington, *Papers*, 9:244-46.

12. Lafayette, *Papers*, 1:88.

13. Ibid., 1:68-78.

14. Friedrich von Muechhausen, *At General Howe's Side, 1776–1778*, trans. Ernst Kipping, ed. Samuel Stelle Smith (Monmouth Beach, NJ: Philip Freneau Press, 1974), 22. This list of British and German troops includes the servants, laborers, and women with the regiments but does not appear to include noncombat military personnel such as the quartermaster's department, hospital, provost, headquarters, etc., for which see Mark Edward Lender and Garry Wheeler Stone, *Fatal Sunday: George Washington, the Monmouth Campaign, and the Politics of Battle* (Norman: University of Oklahoma Press, 2016), 463-70.

15. Washington, *Papers*, 10:518-36, 11:222.

16. Gottschalk, *Lafayette Joins*, 45-59; Lafayette, *Papers*, 1:95-97, 108; Thomas J. McGuire, *The Philadelphia Campaign, Volume I: Brandywine and the Fall of Philadelphia* (Mechanicsburg, PA: Stackpole, 2006), 231-33.

17. Gottschalk, *Lafayette Joins*, 79-83.

18. Washington, *Papers*, 12:466-68, 585-644; Thomas J. McGuire, *The Philadelphia Campaign, Volume II: Germantown and the Roads to Valley Forge* (Mechanicsburg, PA: Stackpole, 2007), 2:241-46.

19. Theodore Thayer, *Nathanael Greene, Strategist of the American Revolution* (New York: Twayne Publishers, 1960), 208-10; Charlemagne Tower, *The Marquis de La Fayette in the American Revolution*, 2nd ed. (Philadelphia: J. B. Lippincott, 1901), 1:245-54; Gottschalk, *Lafayette Joins*, 80-87; Mike Duncan, *Hero of Two Worlds* (NY: PublicAffairs, 2021), 66; Mowday, *Lafayette at Brandywine*, 126-27.

20. Garry Wheeler Stone and Paul W. Schopp, *Gloucester, New Jersey: A Forgotten Battle of the American Revolution*, a report to the American Battlefield Protection Program (grant GA-2287-17-001; Camden, NJ: Camden County Historical Society, September 2019).

CHAPTER 1: THE CONTEXT OF BATTLE: LAND AND PEOPLE

1. John Wilson Croker, *The Croker Papers: The Correspondence and Diaries of the Late Right Honourable John Wilson Croker*, ed. Louis J. Jennings, 2nd ed., 3 vols. (London: John Murray, 1885), 3:276-77.

2. That portion of western Newton Township where the fighting began is now included in the municipalities of Audubon and Haddon Heights.

3. Yeomen were successful farmers, or farmer-craftsmen, able to employ servants. In eighteenth-century South Jersey, the word "plantation" had no size, status, or labor force implications.

4. The earliest topographic map is George H. Cook and C. C. Vermeule, *A Topographic Survey of the Vicinity of Camden to Burlington, Winslow, Elmer and Swedesboro*, Geological Survey of New Jersey, atlas sheet 11 (Trenton: Geological Survey of New Jersey, 1887).

5. Stone and Schopp, *Gloucester*, includes a detailed reconstruction of the battlefield and township. It benefited greatly from David C. Munn, "A Visit to Gloucester Town," unpublished manuscript in the possession of the authors.

6. R. T. Avon Burke and L. L. Lee, *Soil Survey of the Camden Area, New Jersey* (Washington, DC: US Department of Agriculture, 1926); G. M. Hopkins, *Atlas of Philadelphia and Environs* (Philadelphia: G. M. Hopkins, 1877), sheet 20; Cook & Vermeule, *Topographic Survey*, sheet 11; Michel Capitaine du Chesnoy, *Carte de l'action de Gloucester*, Cornell University Library, Division of Rare and Manuscript Collections, Ithaca, NY.

7. Thomas Mann's petition for a tavern license, March 18, 1777, courtesy David Scharf and Patrick Ward.

8. Munn, "Visit," 73-85, includes detailed quotations from the freeholders' minutes documenting the construction and maintenance of the jail and courthouse; Johann Conrad Döhla, *A Hessian Diary of the American Revolution*, ed. Bruce E. Burgoyne (Norman: University of Oklahoma Press, 1990), 60.

9. Munn, "Visit," 88-93; GC, Court of Quarter Sessions and Common Pleas, "Minutes," 5, Dec Term 1771 (pdf image 307); *Pennsylvania Gazette*, June 11, 1767, 4; Aug. 27, 1767, 4; Feb. 16, 1769, 3; May 19, 1773, 3; Jan. 25, 1775, 8; Dec. 22, 1784, 3.

10. George R. Prowell, *History of Camden County, New Jersey* (Philadelphia: L. J. Richards, 1886), 42; NJ, *Minutes of the Provincial Congress and the Council of Safety of New Jersey* (Trenton: Naar, Day & Naar, 1879), 179-81.

11. William Milnor, *An Authentic Historical Memoir of the Schuylkill Fishing Company of the State of Schuylkill . . . with Memoirs of the Gloucester Fox Hunting Club* (Philadelphia: Judah Dobson, 1830); Prowell, *History of Camden County*, 605; *Minutes of the Provincial Council of Pennsylvania*, vol. 10 of the *Colonial Records of Pennsylvania* (Harrisburg: Theo. Fenn, 1852), 282; Wikipedia, s.v. "First Troop Philadelphia City Cavalry" https://en.wikipedia.org/wiki/First_Troop_Philadelphia_City_Cavalry; [John Cadwalader], *Draft of Roads in New Jersey*, MS map, Library of Congress, https://www.loc.gov/resource/g3813c.ar126300/.

12. National Archives, Revolutionary War Pension and Bounty-Land-Warrant Application Files (Microcopy 804), pension file of John Inskeep (W.4703) (hereinafter, pension/pensions); Benjamin Randolph to George Washington, Nov. 15, 1777, in Washington, *Papers*, 12:269-70; William M. Dwyer, *The Day Is Ours* (New York: Viking, 1983), 163-64, 240, 242, 303-304, 347.

13. Prowell, *History of Camden County*, 584-85, 636-40.

14. New Jersey State Archives, ratable books 720, 722, 723, 728 (hereinafter NJSA); NJSA, John Brick Inventory 1298H.

15. Donald M. Londahl-Smidt, "German and British Accounts of the Assault on Fort Mercer at Redbank, NJ, in October 1777," *The Hessians: Journal of the Johannes Schwalm Historical Association* 16 (2013): 13; Christopher Greene, "Orderly Book of Colonel Christopher Greene," New Jersey Society of Pennsylvania, *Year Book for 1928*, 51; Israel Angell, *The Diary of Colonel Israel Angell*, trans. Norman Desmarais, http://digitalcommons.providence.edu/primary/2/, entry for Nov. 1, 1777.

16. William Moraley, *The Infortunate: or, the Voyage and Adventures of William Moraley*, ed. Susan E. Klepp and Billy G. Smith (University Park: Pennsylvania State University Press, 1992), 68 (originally published 1743); Pierre Nicole, *Plan of the City of Philadelphia and Its Environs Shewing Its Defences during the Years 1777 & 1778, together with the Siege of Mud Island*, MS map, Library of Congress, https://www.loc.gov/resource/g3824p.ar132400/. For vegetables, fruit, bread, and chickens marketed in baskets, see the 1759 watercolor paintings of Paul Sandby (British Museum 1872, 1012.3419; National Gallery of Art, USA, 1993.61.1; and many paintings at the Yale Center for British Art). Market baskets

are mentioned in the diary of Job Whitall, *The Diary of Job Whitall of Gloucester County, New Jersey: 1775–1779*, transcribed Florence DeHuff Friel (Woodbury, NJ: Gloucester County Historical Society, 1992); *Pennsylvania Gazette*, Dec. 14, 1774, 5; Feb. 8, 1775, 3.

17. *Pennsylvania Gazette*, Apr. 12 , 1775, 1.

18. NJSA, ratable book 720.

19. Ibid., Probate 493H; Munn, "Visit," 66, 96.

20. NJSA, Gloucester County Deeds 2:55 (hereinafter GC); West Jersey Deeds, N:18-21, 25; NJ, *Acts of the General Assembly of the Province of New-Jersey, 1701–1776*, Samuel Allison, comp. (Burlington, NJ: Isaac Collins, 1776), 156-59; GC, Minutes of the Court of Quarter Sessions & Common Pleas, book 2, Dec. 1714, Mar. 1728; book 3, Sept. 1741, Gloucester County Historical Society (hereinafter GCHS); NJ, *Journal of the Governor and Council*, vol. 3 (1738–1748), ed. Frederick W. Ricord and William Nelson, Archives of the State of New Jersey, 1st ser., 15 (Trenton: John L. Murphy, 1891): 93 (hereinafter ASNJ); NJ, *Journal of the Governor and Council*, vol. 4 (1748–1755), ed. Frederick W. Ricord and William Nelson, ASNJ, 1st ser., 16 (Trenton: John L. Murphy, 1891): 556; Thomas Cushing and Charles E. Sheppard, *History of the Counties of Gloucester, Salem, and Cumberland, New Jersey* (Philadelphia: Everts & Peck, 1883), 122, 124; NJSA, probate 794H, WJ Deeds N:25-27, 475-76.

21. Munn, "Visit," 81; NJSA, ratable book 719; GC, Court of Quarterly Sessions & Common Pleas, Book 4, June Term; William Nelson, ed., *Extracts from American Newspapers*, ASNJ, 1st. ser. (Paterson, NJ: Call, 1903–), 5:613; 6:11; 7:578-79, 588, 8:131.

22. NJ, *Minutes of the Provincial Congress*, 4-23, 169-81; *Pennsylvania Gazette*, July 20, 1774, 3, Dec. 28, 1774, 3; *Pennsylvania Packet*, Dec. 19, 1774, 3; Frank H. Stewart, *Notes on Old Gloucester County, New Jersey*, vol. 3 (Woodbury, NJ: Constitution, 1937), 96-104; *Pennsylvania Archives*, 1st ser., 4 (Philadelphia: Joseph Severns, 1853), 785-86.

23. *Minutes of the Provincial Congress*, 169-99, 325, 446, 471; Cushing and Sheppard, *History*, 123; NJSA, Ratables, 719, 725, 728.

24. NJSA, Auditor's Account A:97, Book B:78, 147, C:38; *Independent Gazetteer* (Philadelphia), Sept. 6, 1783, 3; pensions Martha Harrison (W.4449), Isaac Armstrong (S.2038), William Goforth (R.4091), Stephan Wooley (W.11,880); Heitman, *Officers*, 277; Asher Holmes to Sarah Holmes, Oct. 6, 1777, *Proceedings of the New Jersey Historical Society*, new ser., 7, no. 1 (January 1922): 34-35; Washington, *Papers*, 15:159-61.

25. NJSA, Proprietors of West Jersey, Deed Book B:103; NJSA, Surveys Book H:261-167, S-6:380; NJSA, loose papers, resurvey for William Hugg 1742, no. 60519, resurvey for Jacob Hugg 1742, no. 58143; NJSA, ratable book 720, probates 658H (Jacob Hugg, 1759), 1151H (William Hugg Sr., 1775).

26. Kenn Stryker-Rodda, "New Jersey Rateables, 1773–1774," *Genealogical Magazine of New Jersey* 39, no. 1 (Jan. 1964): 8-9.

27. Cushing and Sheppard, *History*, 123; *Pennsylvania Gazette*, Oct. 5, 1769, 1, Mar. 14, 1771, 4, Jul. 20, 1774, 3, Dec. 21, 1774, 1, Dec. 28, 1774, 3, Apr. 17, 1776; NJ, *Minutes and Proceedings of the Council and General Assembly of the State of New-Jersey in Joint-Meeting, August 30, 1776 to May, 1780* (Trenton, NJ: Isaac Collins, 1780), 7; Job Whitall, *Diary*, 59-62; Records of the Continental and Confederation Congresses, National Archives, Record Group 360 (M247): Remonstrances, 123, 127 (RG 360.2.1); Memorials Addressed to Congress, M (vol. 6):155, 159-61 (RG 360.2.1); Quartermaster's Dept. Letters, 429 (RG 360.2.4); Letters from Colonels, 1776–83, vol. 1, 353 (RG 360.2.4); Washington, *Papers*, 13:30, 601, 14:18-81, 232, 254-55, 416n10; William Livingston, *The Papers of William Livingston*, ed. Carl E. Prince and Dennis P. Ryan (Trenton: New Jersey Historical Commission, 1979–1988), 2:267-68; Jacqueline Thibaut, *This Fatal Crisis: Logistics and the Continental Army at Valley Forge, 1777–1778*, vol. 2 of The Valley Forge Historical Research Report (Valley Forge, PA: Valley Forge National Historical Park, 1982), 122-23, https://www.nps.gov/vafo/learn/historyculture/upload/vol%20ii.pdf.

28. Stone, Hugg Family, https://www.ancestry.com/family-tree/tree/15615 4674/family/familyview?cfpid=282295055740; GC Court, Minutes, 3, March term 1746; NJSA, loose surveys 60519 (Wm. Hugg, 23 Feb. 1741/42); Historic American Building Survey, NJ-282 (Kay House, Bellmawr, NJ) (hereinafter, HABS); *Pennsylvania Gazette*, Apr. 4, 1771, in ASNJ, 1st ser., 27:428.

29. NJSA, loose surveys 60519 (Wm. Hugg, 23 Feb. 1741/42); HABS, NJ-284 (Samuel Hugg House).

30. NJ, *Minutes of the Provincial Congress*, 184, 197, 205, 234, 246, 325, 361-62, 366, 398, 418-19, 439, 492; *Journal of the Proceedings of the Legislative-Council of the State of New-Jersey . . .* convened Oct. 1782 (Trenton: Isaac Collins, 1783), 55; pensions William Johnson (S.33,340), Richard Sayre (I.4660), William Nixon (W.806), Joshua Reeves (S.4759), Hosea Husted (S.34,412), and Reuben Husted (W.465); NJSA, Revolutionary War numbered MS 10568 (Levi Albertson).

31. Pensions John Inskeep (W.4703), Samuel A. Hillman (W.3813, affidavit Jonas Cattell), George Fauver (W.3967); NJSA, numbered MS 10,403; "Meeting of the Gloster Troop" 21 Aug. 1780, Stewart Collection, box 15, folder 49, Special Collections, Campbell Library, Rowan University, Glassboro, NJ; *Proceedings of the New Jersey Historical Society*, 2nd ser., vol. 1 (Newark: Daily Advertiser, 1869), 40-41; *Votes and Proceedings of the General Assembly . . .* begun 26 Oct. 1779 (Trenton: Isaac Collins, 1780), 16; NJSA, numbered MS 5833; Auditor's Book D:321.

32. ASNJ, 1st ser., vol. 22 (*Marriage Records, 1665–1800*), 124; NJSA, Proprietors of West Jersey, Deeds, T:469-70; CCHS, manuscript deeds, Joseph Ellis to George Marple, 1780; ASNJ, 1st ser., 9:184; Thomas B. Wilson, comp., "Records of John Stevens Regarding the New Jersey Regiment in the French & Indian War," 24-25, 32-35 (MS, NJSA); *Pennsylvania Gazette*, 19 Apr 1767, 3; ASNJ, 1st ser., 22:124; William Nelson, *New Jersey Biographical and Genealogical Notes from the Volumes of*

the New Jersey Archives (Newark: New Jersey Historical Society, 1916), 37; NJSA, ratable books 720; GC, Surrogate's Office, Land Division Book 4:1319; GCHS map B-167.

33. Munn, "Visit," 59-61; Nelson, *New Jersey Biographical and Genealogical Notes*, 37; National Register Nomination, Col. Joseph Ellis House, Haddon Heights, Camden County, NJ, copy on file at New Jersey Historic Preservation Office, Trenton; ASNJ, 1st ser., vol. 24 (Newspaper Extracts, 1762–1765): 346.

34. NJSA, ratable book 719; *Pennsylvania Gazette*, July 20, 1774, 3, Dec. 28, 1774, 3; ASNJ, 1st ser., 31:16-17; NJSA, Secretary of State's Office, Liber AB of Commissions, 176, 20 May 1775; NJ, *Minutes of the Provincial Congress*, 184, 197, 205, 234, 246, 325, 353, 361-62, 417, 439; pension Isaac Armstrong (S.2038); John Cadwalader, *A Reply to General Joseph Reed's Remarks on a Late Publication in the Independent Gazetteer* (Philadelphia: T. Bradford, 1783; reprint, ca. 1847–48), 20; "Regimental Returns and Brigade Orders," *Proceedings of the New Jersey Historical Society*, 2nd ser.1:37-40.

35. NJ, *Minutes of the Provincial Congress*, 471, 488-90; Thomas Redman, Thomas Redman's Account of His Being Apprehended & Imprisoned in the Common Gaol at Gloucester, MS, Friends Historical Library, Swarthmore College, Swarthmore, PA.

36. Stone and Schopp, "Gloucester, New Jersey: A Forgotten Battle," unpublished manuscript. Copies on file with the Camden County Historical Society, Camden, NJ, and the American Battlefield Protection Program, National Park Service, Washington, DC.

37. Kenn Stryker-Rodda, "New Jersey Rateables, 1773-1774," *Genealogical Magazine of New Jersey* 39, no. 1 (Jan. 1964): 8; NJSA, ratable books 692, 699.

38. An account of Friends suffering . . . Haddonfield Monthly Meeting, microfilm, Friends Historical Library, Swarthmore College, Swarthmore, PA; Haddonfield Monthly Meeting Marriage Certificates, 1737–1886, 40, Ancestry.com, https://www.ancestry.com/imageviewer/collections/2189/images/31906_2838 28-00291?ssrc=&backlabel=Return; NJSA, ratable books 784, 786, 787, 789.

39. Householders cooked for themselves but owned or rented less than ten acres. Inmate servants ate with their masters or in the master's kitchen.

40. No roster exists for the period during which the McCartys lived in the Town of Gloucester, but after they moved to Newton Township, Dennis McCarty is listed on Captain John Stokes's list (Stewart, *Notes on Old Gloucester County*, 3:31).

41. GC, Minutes Court of Quarter Sessions & Common Pleas, vol. 5 (March 1777): n.p., GCHS.

42. Haddonfield Monthly Meeting, *Minutes*, 3 (1762–1781): 290, 432; An Account of Friends Suffering; 2nd Regiment Gloucester County Militia, regimental orders and courts-martial proceedings, August–September 1780, box 15, folders 26, 49, Frank H. Stewart Collection, Special Collections, Rowan University, Glassboro, NJ.

43. NJSA, West Jersey Deeds AB:218-25.
44. Mount Ephraim Bicentennial Committee, *A History of Mount Ephraim* (Mount Ephraim, NJ: Bicentennial Committee, 1976), no pagination; *Independent Gazetteer*, 6 Sep. 1783, 3; [Cadwalader], *Draft of Roads.*
45. *Pennsylvania Gazette*, Dec. 14, 1774, 5; GC Deeds, PP:147-53.
46. Peter O. Wacker and Paul G. E. Clements, *Land Use in Early New Jersey* (Newark: New Jersey Historical Society, 1995), 218-219.
47. NJSA, ratable books 719, 720, 725, 728.
48. NJSA, probate 1298H; comparison of assessments in ratable books 719, 720, 722, and 728.
49. *Pennsylvania Gazette*, Aug. 21, 1746, 3; Munn, "Visit," 61, 94.
50. NJSA, ratable book 720.

CHAPTER 2: WAR

1. NJ, *Minutes of the Provincial Congress*, 179-81, 187-93, 239; NJ, *Acts of the General Assembly of the State of New-Jersey* (Burlington, NJ: Isaac Collins, 1777), Aug. 1776–Mar 1777, 26-36; May–June 1777, 66-71; Sep.–Oct. 1777, 98-101.
2. Livingston, *Papers*, 1:1-56; Wikipedia, s.v. "William Livingston," https://en.wikipedia.org/wiki/William_Livingston.
3. Barzella Haines to Col. von Donop, 21 Dec. 1776, in David Hackett Fischer, *Washington's Crossing* (New York: Oxford University Press, 2004), 198.
4. George Washington to William Livingston, 24 Jan. 1777, Washington, *Papers*, 8:147-48.
5. GC, Minutes of the Court of Quarter Sessions & Common Pleas, 5 (1771–82): March term 1775, GCHS; GC, Mortgages, A:73-74, GCHS; Heitman, *Officers*, 495; NJ, *Minutes and Proceedings of the Council and General Assembly*), 11, 22; William S. Stryker, *Official Register of the Officers and Men of New Jersey in the Revolutionary War* (Trenton: Wm. T. Nicholson, 1872), 341.
6. Frank H. Stewart, *Notes on Old Gloucester County*, [vol. 1] (Camden: Sinnickson Chew & Sons, 1917), 309-312; NJ, *Minutes and Proceedings of the Council and General Assembly*, 7; Horace Wemyss Smith, *Life and Correspondence of the Rev. William Smith, D.D.* (Philadelphia: Ferguson Bros., 1880), 474-75; Heitman, *Officers*, 422; NJ, *Journal of the Proceedings of the Legislative Council of the State of New-Jersey* (Burlington, NJ: Isaac Collins, 1777), 3; Thomas Redman, Thomas Redman's Account of his being Apprehended & Imprisoned, Friends Historical Library, Swarthmore College; Job Whitall, *Diary*, 50-154, 197.
7. Stewart, *Notes on Old Gloucester County*, 3:106-107; Donald Grady Shomette, *Privateers of the Revolution: War on the New Jersey Coast, 1775–1783* (Atglen, PA: Schiffer, 2016).
8. NJ, *Minutes and Proceedings of the Council and General Assembly*, 7; NJ, *Minutes Provincial Congress*, 197, 325; Stewart, *Notes on Old Gloucester County*, 1:55, 2:102-106; "Regimental Returns and Brigade Orders," *Proceedings of the New Jersey His-*

torical Society, 2nd ser., 1:37; Washington, *Papers*, 11:411-12; Report of Captain Steelman's Company . . . 9 Oct 1778, Col. Richard Somer's Papers, Digital Library, Villanova University, https://library.villanova.edu/Find/Record/vudl:262293.

9. Arthur D. Pierce, *Iron in the Pines* (New Brunswick, NJ: Rutgers University Press, 1957), 118, 123, 179-84; NJSA, ratable books, 665, 673; Stryker-Rodda, "Rateables," 12-16; Stewart, *Notes on Old Gloucester County*, 3:131-32.

10. NJSA, ratable books 690, 804.

11. Ibid., ratable books 719, 649, 804, 805, 784; pension Isaac Armstrong (S.2038); NJSA, Revolutionary War Numbered MS 649; Stone, Stokes Family tree, Ancestry.com.

12. NJSA, Revolutionary War Numbered MS 649; ratable book 784. Mulford had served as a 2nd lieutenant in Col. Silas Newcomb's Regiment of Foot, July to December 1776. See returns, Sept.–Nov. 1776, Revolutionary War Rolls, NA, RG 93 (M246), folder 64.

13. NJSA, ratable book 665; Stryker-Rodda, "Rateables, 1773–1774," 12-14.

14. NJSA, ratable book 673; Stryker-Rodda, "Rateables, 1773–1774," 14-16; ASNJ, 2nd ser., 1:223-24.

15. NJSA, ratable books 665, 673.

16. *Proceedings of the New Jersey Historical Society*, 2nd ser., 1:40-41.

17. Haddonfield Monthly Meeting Minutes, 1762–1781 [vol. 3], 100, 102, 161, 177; "Whitall Family," Friends of the Red Bank Battlefield, https://friendsofred-bank.weebly.com/ uploads/2/3/7/8/23781435/whitall_family.pdf. Benjamin Whitall's willingness to serve may be explained by the diary of his mother, Ann, who once complained that her husband, James, and her sons were casual at best about their Quaker faith. See "Diary of Ann Whitall," Library of Congress transcript, 41-42, https://friendsofredbank.weebly.com/ uploads/2/3/7/8/2378 1435/ann_whitall_diary.pdf.

18. NJ, *Minutes of the Provincial Council*, 549-51; pensions James Tomlin (S.6252) and John Inskeep (W.4703); Newcombs Regiment of Foot 1776 rolls, NA, RG 93 (M246, roll 64), folder 77; Job Whitall, *Diary*, 47-48; Philip Vickers Fithian, *The Beloved Cohansie of Philip Vickers Fithian*, ed. F. Alan Palmer (Greenwich, NJ: Cumberland County Historical Society, 1990), 311-313; Arthur S. Lefkowitz, *The Long Retreat: The Calamitous American Defense of New Jersey 1776* (New Brunswick, NJ: Rutgers University Press, 1999), 35-95.

19. Ewald, *Diary*, 38-44; Johann Emanuel Wagner, Journal of Colonel von Donop, Dec 10–31, 1776, Lingerwood Collection, Morristown National Historical Park, microfiche, letter C, 1- (Boston: G. K. Hall, 1989), 22-28; pension Jeremiah Leeds (S.5686); ASNJ, 2nd ser., 1:243; "Regimental Returns and Brigade Orders," *Proceedings of the New Jersey Historical Society*, 2nd ser., 1:37-40; David Hackett Fischer, *Washington's Crossing* (New York: Oxford University Press, 2004), 271-72, 275-86.

20. Pensions Isaac Armstrong (S.2038), Henry Roe (R.8931).

21. Most of the primary sources for this skirmish have been collected and published. See Glen and Georgeanne Valis, "The Battle of Millstone," http://www.doublegv.com/ggv/battles/millstone.html; Steven M. Richman, "The Battle of Millstone," *Journal of the American Revolution*, Oct. 22, 2014, https://allthingsliberty.com/2014/10/the-battle-of-millstone/.

22. Pensions Jadock Bowen (S.960), Isaac Armstrong (S.2038); NJSA, Auditor's Book B:1, line 2; NJSA, Revolutionary War MS 3933.

23. Pensions Jadock Bowen (S.960), Edward Dowers (S.1278), John Giberson (S.2235), Edward Higbee (R.4971), Jeremiah Leeds (S.5686), Samuel Sooy (3882), James Steelman (S.3985), and Richard Sayres (S.4660).

24. John W. Jackson, *The Pennsylvania Navy, 1775–1781: The Defense of the Delaware* (New Brunswick, NJ: Rutgers University Press, 1965), 12-25.

25. Ibid., 353-76.

26. *Minutes of the Provincial Council of Pennsylvania*, The Colonial Records of Pennsylvania, vol. 10 (Harrisburg: Theo. Fenn, 1852), 282-94 (hereinafter, *Pennsylvania Colonial Records*); *PA Arch*, 1st ser., 4:785-86; Milnor, *Authentic Historical Memoir*, 5, 7, 8, 11, 14, 18.

27. Jackson, *Pennsylvania Navy*, 353-76.

28. Charles E. Peterson, *Robert Smith: Architect, Builder, Patriot 1722–1777* (Philadelphia: Athenæum of Philadelphia, 2000); *Pennsylvania Colonial Records*, 10:474-475, 576, 601-602, 604, 619, 625, 631, 11:6, 19, 56, 125, 139; Heitman, *Officers*, 131.

29. *Pennsylvania Colonial Records*, 10:474-475, 576, 601-602, 604, 619, 625, 631, 11:6, 19, 56, 125, 139; Heitman, *Officers*, 131.

30. Job Whitall, *Diary*, 60-61; Jackson, *Pennsylvania Navy*, 96, 99; *Minutes of the Supreme Executive Council of Pennsylvania*, The Colonial Records of Pennsylvania, vol. 11 (Harrisburg: Theo. Fenn, 1852):248; *PA Arch*, 1st ser., 5:428; NJSA, ratable book 640; NJSA, Revolutionary War Damage Claims, 6.1, microfilm, reel 3, "An acompt of the Damag done to James Whitall;" Du Coudray, "Observations on the Forts," Washington, *Papers*, 10:22-25.

31. NJSA, Auditor's Book B, page 1, lines 10, 11, 25; NJSA Revolutionary War MS 3933, line 33; pensions Nicholas Harris (S.5440, 2 Salem), Joseph Reeves (S.18,563, 2 Cumberland); Du Coudray, "Observations on the Forts," Washington, *Papers*, 10:22-23; *Pennsylvania Colonial Records*, 11:245; Anonymous British Engineer, *Redoubt at Billingsfort and Plan of the Rebel Fort marked Yellow*, MS map, Library of Congress, https://www.loc.gov/resource/g3814p.ar127600/.

32. Muster Roll of Capt. Jacob Ten Eyk's Company, November 1777, NA, RG 93, reel 63.

33. NJ, *Minutes and Proceedings of the Council and General Assembly* 16-19, 24; correspondence between George Washington, Governor William Livingston, and General David Forman, Washington, *Papers*, 12:49-50, 86-87, 135-36, 180-81, 210-11, 470-71.

CHAPTER 3: PRELUDE: TWO ARMIES CONVERGE ON THE DELAWARE VALLEY

1. Naval History and Heritage Command, *Naval Documents of the American Revolution*, vol. 9 (Washington, DC: Naval Historical Center, 1986), 354, 362-63 (hereinafter *NDAR*); Ambrose Serle, *The Journal of Ambrose Serle, Secretary to Lord Howe*, ed. Edward H. Tatum Jr. (San Marino, CA: 1940), 240-246; John Montresor, *The Montresor Journals, Collections of the New-York Historical Society for the Year 1882*, ed. G. D. Scull (New York: New-York Historical Society, 1882), 426-49.

2. McGuire, *The Philadelphia Campaign*, 1:263-329; Friedrich von Muenchhausen, *At General Howe's Side, 1776–1779*, trans. Ernst Kipping, ed. Samuel Stelle Smith (Monmouth Beach, NJ: Philip Freneau Press, 1974), 36; Sarah Logan Fisher, "'A Diary of Trifling Occurrences,' Philadelphia, 1776–1778," ed. Nicholas B. Wainwright, *PMHB* 82, no. 4 (Oct 1958): 450.

3. Muenchhausen, *General Howe's Side*, 36-41; Montresor, *Journals*, 462-472.

4. Stephen Kemble, *Journals of Lieut. Col. Stephen Kemble, 1773–1789; and British Army orders: Gen. Sir William Howe, 1775–1778; Gen. Sir Henry Clinton, 1778; and Gen. Daniel Jones, 1778* (Boston: Greg Press, 1972), 507; John Peebles, *John Peebles' American War: The Diary of a Scottish Grenadier, 1776–1782*, ed. Ira D. Gruber (Mechanicsburg, PA: Stackpole, 1998), 140-41; Archibald Robertson, *Archibald Robertson: His Diaries and Sketches in America, 1762–1780*, ed. Harry Miller Lydenberg (New York: New York Public Library, 1930), 151; Muenchhausen, *Howe's Side*, 38, 73-74; *NDAR*, 9:983, 10:12, 13, 29.

5. *NDAR*, 10:29; Jackson, *Pennsylvania Navy*, 86, 128; pension declarations of Joseph Reeves (S.18,565), Charles Simpkins (R.9588), and Samuel Westcott (S.1145); NJSA, Auditor's Book B:1, lines 22, 39.

6. *NDAR*, 10:29; NJSA, Auditor's Book B:145, line 1; pension Franklin Davenport (S.2508). Samuel Hugg supervised the field piece the prior month. Hugg's Artillery Payroll, September 1777, *Proceedings of the New Jersey Historical Society*, 2nd ser., 1:40-41.

7. Peebles, *American War*, 194; Robertson, *Diaries and Sketches*, 151; *NDAR*, 10:29; pensions Charles Simpkins (R.9588), Joseph Reeves (S.18,565), Samuel Westcott (S.1145); pension Thomas McGee (S.5752) transcribed and annotated by C. Leon Harris, Southern Campaigns Revolutionary War Pension Statements & Rosters, revwarapps.org.

8. *NDAR*, 10:29; *PA Arch*, 1st ser., 5:644-45.

9. *NDAR*, 10:29.

10. Peebles, *American War*, 194; *NDAR*, 10:29, 39, 44.

11. Samuel Smith to George Washington, 2 Oct. 1777, Washington, *Papers*, 11:368.

12. George Washington to James Mitchell Varnum, October 7, 1777, Washington, *Papers*, 11:427.

13. George Washington to John Hazelwood, October 7, 1777, Washington, *Papers*, 11:422, 437; Jackson, *Pennsylvania Navy*, 439n74; Heitman, *Officers*, 168; National Archives, Record Group 93 (M246, roll 120), folder 56:2; John Smith, "'Thro Mud & Mire into the Woods': The 1777 Continental Army Diary of Sergeant John Smith, First Rhode Island Regiment," ed. Bob McDonald, Rev War'75.com, http://www.revwar75.com/library/bob/smith.htm.

14. Ellis's contingent appears to have included Captain Richard Cheesman's 1st Gloucester Company. Mustering with Cheesman was a young Deptford man, Jonas Cattell, at that time a blacksmith's apprentice in Haddonfield, Newton Township. Pension Jonas Cattell (S.2421) and James Davis's affidavit. Also, Cattell's affidavit for Mary Hillman (W.3813).

15. NJSA, Auditor's Book B: p. 1, line 11, p. 2, line 57; Washington, *Papers*, 11:503-504.

16. Greene, "Orderly Book," 48-50; Smith, *Diary*; Washington, *Papers*, 11:437-38, 12:287; NJSA, Revolutionary War Damage Claims, 6.1 (microfilm, reel 3), "An acompt of the Damag done to James Whitall"; François Jean de Beauvoir, marquis de Chastellux, *Travels in North-America in the Years 1780–81–82* (New York: 1828), 125; Jackson, *Pennsylvania Navy*, 146-54, Jeremiah Greenman, *Diary of a Common Soldier of the American Revolution, 1775–1783*, ed. Robert C. Bray and Paul E. Bushnell (DeKalb: Northern Illinois University Press, 1978), 82.

17. Washington, *Papers*, 11:567, 577-78; pension Richard Tice (S.28,912).

18. Washington, *Papers*, 11:581-82; Heitman, *Officers*, 105; Smith, *Diary*; Greene, "Orderly Book," 49-50.

19. Washington, *Papers*, 11:581-82; Smith, *Diary*; Job Whitall, *Diary*, 80-81.

20. Greenman, *Diary*, 81-82; Smith, *Diary*; Washington, *Papers*, 11:559-60; pension Isaac Smith (W.4338), transcribed and annotated by C. Leon Harris, Southern Campaigns Revolutionary War Pension Statements & Rosters, revwarapps.org; Edwin Martin Stone, "The Invasion of Canada in 1775: Including the Journal of Captain Simeon Thayer, with Notes and Appendix," *Collections of the Rhode Island Historical Society* 6 (1867): 75.

21. Pension Jonas Cattell (S.2421); Jonas Cattell, "Reminiscences," *The Constitution*, Woodbury, NJ, 10 Mar. 1846, http://www.jonascattell.com/cattell.html; Washington, *Papers*, 11:581-82; Londahl-Smidt, "German and British Accounts," 19 ("a few popping shots").

22. Londahl-Smidt, "German and British Accounts," 6, 13, 15, 27; Jackson, *Pennsylvania Navy*, 173, 190; Smith, *Diary*, 1 Nov.; Greene, "Orderly Book," 51.

23. Londahl-Smidt, "German and British Accounts," 6, 11, 16, 27; Cadwalader, *Draft of Roads*. Arrival times at Fort Mercer stated in the Hessian accounts vary radically, from 10:00 am to 2:00 pm. The chronology given in the text is based on our collation of all the available information.

24. Londahl-Smidt, "German and British Accounts," 1-33.

25. Ibid.; *NDAR,* 8:634, 675, 10:245-54, 260-63, 289-93, 304-308, 370, 386.

26. Smith, *Diary,* Oct. 23, Nov. 1, 1777; Greene, "Orderly Book," 51.

27. Montresor, *Journals,* 474.

28. Worthington Chauncey Ford, "The Defences of Philadelphia in 1777," *PMHB* 19 (1935): 85-86, 236-38, 241-48, 361-71; *NDAR,* 10:467, 472, 478, 489, 492-93; Montresor, *Journals,* 474-76.

29. Francis Downman, *The Services of Lieut.-Colonel Francis Downman, R.A.,* ed. Colonel F. A. Whinyates (London: Royal Artillery Institution, 1898), 51-52.

30. George Washington to Henry Laurens, 17–18 Nov. 1777, Washington, *Papers,* 12:295.

31. Von Knyphausen to Landgrave, 30 Nov. 1777, Letter G, fiche no. 56:127, 130, Lidgerwood Collection, Morristown National Historical Park, Morristown, NJ; George Weedon to Nathanael Greene, 24 Nov. 1777, *The Papers of General Nathanael Greene,* ed. Richard K. Showman (Chapel Hill: University of North Carolina Press, 1980), 2:214.

32. Robertson, *Diaries and Sketches,* 156; James Pattison, *The James Pattison Papers, 1777–1781,* ed. I. F. Burton (London: Royal Artillery Institution, 1963), 15; *NDAR,* 10:543; Washington, *Papers,* 12:324; Frank H. Stewart, *History of the Battle of Red* Bank (Woodbury, NJ: Gloucester County Freeholders, 1927), 21; the Mantua Creek skirmish probably is the one remembered by David Somers of Egg Harbor Township, pension S.4868.

33. Washington, *Papers,* 12:286-87, 304-307, 313, 322-23; *NDAR,* 10:522.

34. Washington, *Papers,* 12:316-17, 321-23. Troop strengths are from Charles H. Lesser, ed., *The Sinews of Independence: Monthly Strength Reports of the Continental Army* (Chicago: University of Chicago Press, 1976), 53. Most are from 3 Dec. 1777, while the report for Huntington's Brigade is from 16 Nov. 1777.

35. Lafayette, *Papers,* 1:155.

36. Robertson, *Diaries,* 156; Julius Stirke, "A British Officer's Revolutionary War Journal," ed. S. Sydney Bradford, *Maryland Historical Magazine* 54 (1961): 150-175; John W. Jackson, *The Pennsylvania Navy, 1775–1781: The Defense of the Delaware* (New Brunswick: Rutgers University Press, 1965), 272-78.

CHAPTER 4: BATTLE: LAFAYETTE'S "LITTLE EVENT"

1. Pattison, *Papers,* 25-26; Freyenhagen, "Journal," 70.

2. Robertson, *Diaries and Sketches,* 156; Stephan Popp, *A Hessian Soldier in the American Revolution,* trans. Reinhart J. Pope (privately printed, 1953), 8.

3. Job Whitall, *Diary,* 85. Most of the cattle escaped and came back.

4. Ibid., 85-86.

5. *Jackson's Oxford Journal* (UK), 17 Jan. 1778, 1, Newspapers.com.

6. Robertson, *Diaries and Sketches,* 157; Stirke, "Journal," 175.

7. Prowell, *History of Camden County,* 58; HABS NJ-282.

8. Stirke, "Journal," 175; Stephen Gilbert, "Light Infantry in New Jersey, Pennsylvania, and New York, 1777–1778," chap. 3 in "British Light Infantry" (unpublished manuscript last modified March 2020), n.p. The fatalities were Privates Stephen Sutton and John Key.

9. Pensions Samuel Asay (R.273); Robert Leeds, Capt. Payne's Coy., Egg Harbor Township, Gloucester County (S.18489); and from Cumberland County, Charles Simpkins (R.9588), and Jeremiah Towser (S.6254); Robertson, *Diaries and Sketches*, 157.

10. Freyenhagen, "Journal," 71; Montresor, *Journals*, 479; *NDAR*, 10:595; Rif Winfield, *British Warships in the Age of Sail, 1714–1792* (Barnsley, UK: Seaforth, 2007), 334.

11. Washington, *Papers*, 12:169, 175, 210, 232, 266, 273, 13: 247, 296, 352; Livingston, *Papers*, 2:96-100, 102-103, 110, 129, 567.

12. Stewart, *Notes on Old Gloucester County*, 3:25-31,102-106; Shomette, *Privateers*, 23-27; NJSA, Revolutionary War MS 3904, Payroll Jacob Ten Eyk, Nov. 1777, NA, RG 93, reel 63.

13. Greene, *Papers*, 2:204; Washington, *Papers*, 12:93.

14. Wikipedia, "Long rifle," https://en.wikipedia.org/wiki/Long_rifle. For James Knox, see Lewis and Richard H. Collins, *History of Kentucky* (Covington, KY: Collins, 1874), 2:417-18, 517.

15. Harry M. Ward, *When Fate Summons: A Biography of General Richard Butler* (Bethesda, MD: Academica Press, 2014), 1-17, 125-26; Richard Butler, deposition, 23 Aug. 1774, *Pennsylvania Archives*, ser. 1, 4:568-70.

16. Donald B. Kiddoo, "Major Joseph Morris in Action," A Veteran's Day Tribute presented by the First Presbyterian Church, Whippany, North Jersey History Center, Morristown and Morris Township Library; *The Record, the History of the First Presbyterian Church of Morristown* 5, no. 34 (Oct. 1885): 182-84, no. 35 (Nov. 1885): 185; Oscar Jewell Harvey, *A History of Wilkes-Barré, Luzerne County, Pennsylvania* (Wilkes-Barré: Raeder Press, 1909), 1:514, 2:625-29, 694-709; William C. Armstrong, *Pioneer Settlers of Northeastern New Jersey* (Lambertville, NJ: Hunterdon House, 1979), 330-36, 378-83; NJ, *Minutes of the Provincial Congress*, 104-106; Stryker, *Official Register*, 9-13; Heitman, *Officers*, 403; Washington, *Papers*, 8:319, 9:270-71; James Wilkinson, *Memoirs of My Own Times* (Philadelphia: Abraham Small, 1816), 1:236-38.

17. Higginbotham, *Daniel Morgan*, 57-65; Henry Dearborn, *Revolutionary War Journals of Henry Dearborn,* ed. Lloyd A. Brown and Howard H. Peckham (Chicago: Caxton Club, 1939), 103-105; Richard M. Ketchum, *Saratoga* (New York: Henry Holt, 1997), 341-55; Brendan Morrissey, *Saratoga 1777* (Oxford: Osprey, 2000), 57-59.

18. Israel Trask, pension, in John C. Dann, *The Revolution Remembered: Eyewitness Accounts of the War for Independence* (Chicago: University of Chicago Press, 1980), 406-409; David Hackett Fischer, *Washington's Crossing* (New York: Oxford Uni-

versity Press, 2004), 22-25; Richard B. LaCrosse Jr., *Revolutionary Rangers* (Westminster, MD: Heritage Books, 2002), 23, 98.

19. Arno Störkel, "The Ansback Jägers," *The Hessians*, 14 (2011): 1-31.

20. Everett K. Spees, "Hessen-Cassel Erbprinz Fusilier Regiment Prepares and Departs of America–1776," *The Hessians*, 22 (2019): 16-37; Johann Ewald, *Diary of the American Revolution*, ed. Joseph P. Tustin (New Haven, CT: Yale University Press, 1979), 7-17.

21. Ewald, *Diary*, xix-xxxi; Rang—Liste (rank list, Sept. 1777), Jäger, Feldjäger Corps 1777 Monatl. Listen, Bestand 15, vol. 160, fol. 13a, Hessisches Staatsarchiv Marburg. Transcription provided by Donald M. Londahl-Smidt.

22. *NDAR*, 9:25; Störkel, "Ansback Jägers," 6; Bruce E. Burgoyne, trans., Bruce E. Burgoyne and Marie E. Burgoyne, eds., *Journal of the Hesse-Cassel Jaeger Corps and Hans Konze's List of Jaeger Officers* (Westminster, MD: Heritage Books, 2008), 1-3; Ewald, *Diary*, 64-69; Von Muenchhausen, *At Howe's Side*, 12-20 (new jägers, 13, 16, 19).

23. Ewald, *Diary*, 71-78; Burgoyne and Burgoyne, *Jäger Journal and Officers*, 7-8; Von Muenchhausen, *At Howe's Side*, 28; McGuire, *Philadelphia Campaign*, 1:152-58.

24. Burgoyne and Burgoyne, *Jäger Journal*, 25-29; Ewald, *Diary*, 105; Lt. Gen. Wilhelm von Knyphausen to Landgrave, 30 Nov. 1777, Letter G, fiche 56:130, 134-35, transcripts and translation from the Lidgerwood Collection, Morristown National Historical Park, reference courtesy Donald Londahl-Smidt.

25. Greene, *Papers*, 2:202-214; John Hills, *A Sketch of Haddonfield, West New Jersey County*, Henry Clinton Papers, Brun Guide 584, William L. Clements Library, Ann Arbor, Michigan.

26. Greene, *Papers*, 2:207.

27. Ibid., 2:214.

28. Major William Blodget to General George Weedon, 24 Nov. 1777, Gilder Lehrman Collection, https://www.gilderlehrman.org/collection/glc0649802; Greene, *Papers*, 2:214; Robertson, *Diaries and Sketches*, 157; Pattison, *Papers*, 15; Cushing and Sheppard, *History*, 540.

29. Robertson, *Diaries and Sketches*, 157; Greene, *Papers*, 2:214-15, Lafayette, *Papers*, 1:156.

30. Greene, *Papers*, 2:214-15. The "Hessian General" was neither Hessian nor a general. He was either Colonel Friedrich Ludwig Albrecht von Eyb, commander of the 1st Ansbach-Bayreuth Regiment, or the 2nd Regiment commander, Colonel August Valentin von Voit von Salzburg. Döhla, *Hessian Diary*, xviii.

31. Greene, *Papers*, 2:215; pensions Robert Leeds (S.18,489), David Somers (S.4868); Johann Christoph Doehlemann, "Diary of Johann Christoph Doehlemann, Grenadier Company, Ansbach Regiment, March 1777 to September 1778," transcribed Karl Walther, trans. Henry J. Retzer, *The Hessians*, 11 (2008): 15.

32. Lafayette, *Papers*, 1:156.

33. Washington, *Papers*, 12:419.

34. Gloucester County deed research by Garry Stone. For Newton Meeting House, see Robert Shinn, Andrew Levecchia, and Sandra White Grear, "The Newton Union Burial Ground," *SoJourn* (Winter 2018/19).

35. Newton Township ratable book, Feb. 1779, NJSA, book 784; *Pennsylvania Gazette*, Mar. 2, 1769, Mar. 8, 1770, Nov. 21, 1771.

36. Du Chesnoy, *Carte de l'action de Gloucester*. The sand hill is shown on Cook and Vermeule, *Topographic Survey*. The sand hill was leveled in 1906. *Philadelphia Inquirer*, 18 Mar. 1906, information from Patrick Ward; Lafayette, *Papers*, 1:156; Greene, *Papers*, 2:214.

37. Lafayette, *Papers*, 1:156; Capitaine, *l'action de Gloucester*; Greene, *Papers*, 2:214; Washington, *Papers*, 12:343.

38. Lafayette, *Papers*, 1:156-58.

39. Heitman, *Officers*, 73; Washington to Charles Armand-Tuffin, Marquis de la Rouerie, 15 Dec. 1783, Library of Congress, George Washington Papers, ser. 2, letterbook 11; NA, Revolutionary War Rolls, RG 93 (M246), 1st Continental Light Dragoons, folder 7:3-4 (Lee's Fifth Troop, Dec. 1777), folder 5:6-7 (Dandridge's 3rd Troop, Nov. 1777); NA, Compiled Service Records (M881) for Lieutenant William Lindsay; Auditor's Book B:135, line 28.

40. Pensions John A. Auten (S.945), Jadock Bowen (S.960), Jesse Conover (S.2462), Robert Leeds (S18,489), Jacob Matlock (S.2756), Patrick McCollum (S.2768), Joshua Reeves (S.29,404), Richard Sayres (S.4660), Richard Tice (S.28,912); Stryker, *Official Register*, 389; NJSA, Revolutionary War MS 10, 222.

41. Greene, *Papers*, 2:215; pension John A. Auten (S.945). Auten's pension declaration provides the best account of the march.

42. Pension John A. Auten (S.945).

43. "Journal of Ensign/Lt. Wilhelm Johann Ernst Freyenhagen Jr.—1776–1778," trans. Henry J. Retzer, annot. Donald M. Londahl-Smidt, *The Hessians* 14 (2011): 71.

44. Freyenhagen, "Journal," 14:71; Hessian transcripts, Letter G, fiche no. 56:128-129, Lidgerwood Collection, Morristown National Historical Park.

45. September 3, 1777, von Wrede's and Ewald's jäger companies had driven rifle-armed Continental light infantry from Iron Hill, DE, with rifle and hunting sword (Ewald, *Diary*, 78; McGuire, *Philadelphia Campaign*, 1:149-56.

46. Lafayette, *Papers*, 1:156; Freyenhagen, "Journal,"14:71; Hessian transcripts, Letter G, fiche no. 56:128, Lidgerwood Collection, Morristown National Historical Park.

47. Cushing and Sheppard, *History*, 540; pensions Robert Leeds (S.18,489), John Tilton (S.581), Joshua Reeves (S.29,404), Ephraim Simkins (S.4673), John Auten (S.945).

48. Pension Richard Sayres (S.4660).

49. Ephraim Albertson is interred in the Sloan burial ground with Friends who had been read out of meeting for participating in the Revolution. Shinn, Levecchia, and Grear, "Newton Union Burial Ground."

50. Lafayette, *Papers*, 1:157.

51. Ibid., 1:156. For militia musicians who served at Haddonfield, see pensions Richard Tice (S.28912) and Levi Price (S.3733).

52. Lafayette, *Papers*, 1:157; *ASNJ*, 2nd ser., 1:497.

53. Freyenhagen, "Journal," 71.

54. Personal communication from military historian Stephen Gilbert, 25 Mar. 2020.

55. Lafayette, *Papers*, 1:156-57.

56. Cushing and Sheppard, *History*, 540.

57. Pension Patrick McCollum (S.2768). Warm clothes were wasted on a corpse. After the failed October attack on Fort Mercer, the Continentals stripped the bodies of all enlisted men, Continental as well as Hessian. British grenadiers, after occupying Fort Mifflin, salvaged clothing from the bodies of the dead Continentals. Smith, *Diary*, 23 Oct. 1777; Downman, *Services*, 52; Cattell, "Reminiscences," http://www.jonascattell.com/cattell.html.

58. NJSA, Revolutionary War MS 10222, 10192, 10568, 10212; *Votes and Proceedings* (1780), 41; *Votes and Proceedings of the Twenty-Second General Assembly* (Trenton, NJ: Matthias Day, 1797), 13.

59. Pensions Richard Tice (28,912), Nehemiah Dean (S. 866), and Berung VanDoren (S.4694). John Fields (S.8472) of Burlington County also remembered fighting under a Frenchman, but he may have been remembering du Plessis.

60. Among the pension declaration extracts provided Schopp and Stone by Jason R. Wickersty are eighteen from South Jersey that included references to the 25 Nov. 1777 skirmish. Sixteen of the eighteen cite the loss of Lucas or Mulford; many also list men who had been wounded.

61. Lafayette, *Papers*, 1:158.

62. Greene, *Papers*, 2:218-19.

63. Ibid., 2:219-23; Johann Ernst Prechtel, *A Hessian Officer's Diary*, trans. Bruce E. Burgoyne (Westminster, MD: Heritage Books, 1994), 14; Döhla, *Diary*, 60; Paul W. Schopp, "Historic Cultural Context," pt. 4, 34–42, in New Jersey Department of Transportation, I-295/I-76/Route 42 Direct Connection, Phase I/II Archaeological Investigation Technical Environmental Study, vol. 1, March 2006, http://www.state.nj.us/transportation/commuter/roads/rt295/pdf/PhaseI-IIArchaeoInvestTESVol_I.pdf.

64. Greene, *Papers*, 2:221-23; Freyenhagen, "Journal," 71.

65. Greene, *Papers*, 2:222-25.

66. John André, *Major André's Journal*, ed. Henry Cabot Lodge (Tarrytown, NY: William Abbatt, 1930), 66; Montresor, *Journals*, 479; Stirke, "Journal," 175; pension John A. Auten (S.945).

67. Freyenhagen, *Journal*, 71; Montresor, *Journals*, 479. In addition, schooner *Viper* fired five rounds, *NDAR*, 10:617.

68. Pension Jadock Bowen (S.960); Richard Butler to James Wilson, Jan. 22, 1778, Historical Society of Pennsylvania, Gratz Collection, Case 4, Box 11, reference courtesy of Patrick Ward, GCityHS.

69. The burned plantations were those of commissaries Joseph Hugg and Israel Morris. See chapters 2 and 4 above. For Cornwallis's troops' behavior in an occupied village, see Job Whitall's description of the plundering of Woodbury. *Diary*, 85-86.

70. Captain von Wrede's list of casualties was enclosed in Knyphausen's report to Friedrich II, 30 Nov. 1777, Bestand 4h, Nr. 3099, fol. 132, Hessisches Staatsarchiv Marburg; Inge Auerbachand Otto Fröhlich, *Hessische Truppen im Amerikanischen*, vol. 4 (Marburg, Germany: Archivschule Marburg, 1976), also at http://www.lagis-hessen.de/en/subjects/index/sn/hetrina. Transcriptions of both documents provided by Donald M. Londahl-Smidt; Stewart, *Notes on Old Gloucester County*, 3:35-36.

71. John André, *Major André's Journal*, 66; Montrésor, *Journals*, 479; Peebles, *American War*, 151; Stirke, "Journal," 175.

72. *Letters of Delegates to Congress, 1774-1789*, ed. Paul H. Smith, vol. 8 (Washington, DC: Library of Congress, 1981), 346-47, 368, 375; Washington, *Papers*, 12:439, 443, 456.

73. Lafayette, *Papers*, 1:156-58; Lafayette to Butler, *PMHB*, 14, no. 1 (1890), 83; Greene, *Papers*, 2:200.

74. See Lafayette's letters to Washington, Mar.–Aug. 1781, especially Mar. 26, Apr. 23, May 24, July 20, at https://founders.archives.gov/documents/Washington; *Papers of Alexander Hamilton*, vol. 2 (1779–1781), ed. Harold C. Syrett (New York: Columbia University Press, 1961), 518-21, 587-89, 592-93; and St. George Tucker's description of the reunion of Lafayette and Washington, 14 Sep. 1781, in Mary Haldane Coleman, *St. George Tucker: Citizen of No Mean City* (Richmond, VA: Dietz Press, 1938), 70.

CHAPTER 5: THE PROMOTION OF MAJOR GENERAL THE MARQUIS DE LAFAYETTE

1. Washington, *Papers*, 11:4-5, 13; Lafayette, *Papers*, 1:86n17, 88; Gottschalk, *Lafayette Joins*, 22-38.

2. Lafayette, *Papers*, 1:121-24, 146, 152-55.

3. Washington, *Papers*, 12:81.

4. Ibid., 12:408-11, 417-20.

5. Ibid., 12:420-21.

6. *Letters of Delegates*, 8:345-47, 351, 363.

7. Lafayette, *Papers*, 1:156-61, 65; Washington, *Papers*, 12:408-411, 417-22; Worthington Chauncey Ford, ed., *Journals of the Continental Congress, 1774-1789*, vol. 9

(Washington, DC: Government Printing Office, 1907), 982-83; *Virginia Gazette*, 19 Dec. 1777, 1; Purdie's *Virginia Gazette*, 19 Dec. 1777, 4; *Maryland Gazette*, 18 Dec. 1777, 1; *Pennsylvania Packet*, 24 Dec. 1777, 4.

8. Washington, *Papers*, 12:534, Lender and Stone, *Fatal Sunday*, 390-403.

9. Harry M. Ward, *Major General Adam Stephen and the Cause of American Liberty* (Charlottesville: University Press of Virginia, 1989), 2-175; Lender, *Cabal*, 45-48, 60-61.

10. McGuire, *Philadelphia Campaign*, 2:97-99, 120-22; Ward, *Stephen*, 176-196.

11. Washington, *Papers*, 11:330, 468-71, 605-606, 12:91-92, 276-77, 327-28; McGuire, *Philadelphia Campaign*, 2:98-99, 120-22, 177; Ward, *Stephen*, 197-207; Greene, *Papers*, 2:188; *Letters of Delegates*, 8:339.

12. Washington, *Papers*, 11:507.

13. Charles H. Lesser, ed., *The Sinews of Independence* (Chicago: University of Chicago Press, 1976), 54; NA, RG 93, M246, reel 133, folder 226.

14. McGuire, *Philadelphia Campaign*, 2:239-56; Honors History 12, *Driving Tour of the Battle of Whitemarsh*, ed. Thomas Sorkness (Erdenheim, PA: Philadelphia-Montgomery Christian Academy, 2017), 16, https://battleofwhitemarsh.weebly.com/.

15. Lafayette, *Papers*, I:183-87.

16. Washington, Papers, 12:589-90, 608, 612-13, 685, 695, 13:17, 37, 42; Lafayette, *Papers*, 1:199-201.

17. Lafayette, *Papers*, 1:193-94.

18. Pensions Jesse Conover (S.2462), Edward Dowers (S.2178), Nicholas Harris (S.5440), Patrick McCollum (S.2768), and Samuel Bowen (S.22,133).

19. Pensions Anthony Crockett (S.10,492, transcribed by Will Graves) and James Barnett (W.391), transcribed by C. Leon Harris, Southern Campaigns Revolutionary War Pension Statements & Rosters, revwarapps.org.

20. Lafayette, *Papers*, 2:6-17, 43, 48-49, 172-76, 185-86; Washington, *Papers*, 15:4-5, 33-40, 79-81, 151-54; Gottschalk, *Lafayette Joins*, 271-83; Lender and Stone, *Fatal Sunday*, 76-104, 123-354.

21. Lafayette, *Papers*, 2:186-87, 190-96; John C. Fitzpatrick, ed., *The Writings of George Washington* (Washington, DC: Government Printing Office, 1936), 13:40-41.

22. Lafayette, *Papers*, 2:190-98, 217-29, George Washington to Benjamin Franklin, Dec. 28, 1778, https://founders.archives.gov/documents/Washington/03-18-02-0584; Gottschalk, *Lafayette Joins*, 289-305, 313-27.

23. Lafayette, *Papers*, 2:199-200; Gottschalk, *Lafayette Comes*, 85, 88, 92.

24. Lafayette, *Papers*, 2:200-201; "A Sword for the Marquis de Lafayette," Founders Online, https://founders.archives.gov/documents/Franklin/01-30-02-0203.

25. For a contemporary description of the work and products of the *fourbisseur*, see Dennis Diderot, *Encyclopédie ou Dictionnaire raisonné des sciences, des arts et des métiers, par une Société de Gens de lettres*, vol. 4 (Paris, 1754). Four of the illustrations

are reproduced in Charles Coulston Gillispie, ed., *A Diderot Pictorial Encyclopedia of Trades and Industry* (New York: Dover, 1959), 1, plates 181-84.

26. Christian M. McBurney, "Presentation Swords for 10 Revolutionary War Heroes," *Journal of the American Revolution*, May 16, 2014, https://allthingsliberty.com/2014/05/presentation-swords-for-ten-revolutionary-war-heroes.

27. Lafayette, *Papers*, 2:226-53, 258-71, 284-87, 291-92, 304-305; Louis Gottschalk, *Lafayette and the Close of the American Revolution* (Chicago: University of Chicago Press, 1942, 1965), 1-50; Jules Cloquet, *Recollections of the Private Life of General Lafayette* (New York: Leavitt, Lord, 1836), 2:9, 12.

28.. Lafayette, *Papers*, 2:303-305; NA, RG 360 (M247, roll 72), Papers of the Continental Congress, item 59 (Misc. Papers, 1770–89), 1:33-38; Bank of England Inflation Calculator, https://www.bankofengland.co.uk/monetary-policy/inflation/inflation-calculator; John J. McCusker, "How Much Is That in Real Money? A Historical Price Index," *Proceedings of the American Antiquarian Society* 101, pt. 2 (Oct. 1991): 297-373.

29. Lafayette, *Papers*, 2:303-304; "Sword for the Marquis," document 3; Benjamin Franklin to John Jay, Oct. 4, 1779, in *The Works of Benjamin Franklin*, ed. John Bigelow (New York: G.P. Putnam's Sons, 1904), vol. 8, Letters and Miscellaneous Writings, 1779–1781, Online Library of Liberty, https://oll.libertyfund.org/title/franklin-the-works-of-benjamin-franklin-vol-viii-letters-and-misc-writings-1779-1781#lf1438-08_head_068.

30. Lafayette, *Papers*, 2:304-309.

31. "Sword for the Marquis," document 1.

32. Sword cutler Liger described the sword as an *"Epéé Dor a Bataille"* in the receipt he gave Franklin ("A Sword for the Marquis," document 2). The misspellings of *épeé* and *d'or* are Liger's. *The Papers of John Adams*, Series 3: General and Public Correspondence, vol. 8, March 1779–February 1780, ed. Gregg L. Lint et al. (Cambridge, MA: Harvard University Press, 1989); Adams Papers Digital Edition, https://www.masshist.org/publications/adams-papers/index.php/view/ADMS-06-08-02-0254.

EPILOGUE

1. Gottschalk, *Lafayette Joins the American Army* (Chicago: University of Chicago Press, 1965); Louis Gottschalk, *Lafayette and the Close of the American Revolution* (Chicago: University of Chicago Press, 1942, 1965); Harlow Giles Unger, *Lafayette* (Hoboken, NJ: John Wiley & Sons, 2002).

2. Unger, *Lafayette*, 196-204; Lafayette, *Papers*, 5:240-41, 271-87.

3. Auguste Levasseur, *Lafayette in America in 1824 and 1825*, trans. John D. Godman, 2 vols. (Philadelphia: Carey and Lea, 1829), 1:10-11.

4. Ibid., vols. 1 and 2.

5. Ibid., 2:241-56; John Quincy Adams, *Memoirs of John Quincy Adams, Comprising Portions of His Diary from 1795 to 1848*, ed. Charles Francis Adams, 12 vols.

(Philadelphia: J. B. Lippincott, 1874–77), 7:39-50; Nolan J. Bennett, *Lafayette in America, Day by Day* (Baltimore: Johns Hopkins University Press, 1934), 300-305.

6. Unger, *Lafayette*, 370-80; Biography, s.v. "Marquis de Lafayette," https://www.biography.com/political-figure/marquis-de-lafayette.

7. Wikipedia, s.v. "List of Places Named for the Marquis de Lafayette," https://en.wikipedia.org/wiki/List_of_places_named_for_the_Marquis_de_Lafayette.

8. Wikipedia, s.v. "Charles E. Stanton," https://en.wikipedia.org/wiki/Charles_E._Stanton.

Bibliography

MANUSCRIPT COLLECTIONS

Adams Family Papers. Massachusetts Historical Society, Boston.

Angell, Israel. The Diary of Colonel Israel Angell. Massachusetts Historical Society, Boston.

Butler, Richard. Richard Butler to James Wilson, January 22, 1778. Simon Gratz Collection, Pennsylvania Historical Society, Philadelphia.

Clement, John. John Clement Collection, Maps and Drafts. Pennsylvania Historical Society, Philadelphia.

Clinton, Henry. Papers. William L. Clements Library, University of Michigan, Ann Arbor, MI.

Continental Army. Revolutionary War Pension and Bounty-Land-Warrant Application Files. Record Group 15, Microfilm 804, National Archives, Washington, DC.

———. Revolutionary War Rolls, 1775–1783. Record Group 93, Microfilm 246, National Archives, Washington, DC.

———. Revolutionary War Compiled Service Records, 1775–1783, Record Group 93, Microfilm M881, National Archives, Washington, DC.

Continental Congress. Papers of the Continental Congress, 1774–1789. Record Group 360, Microfilm 247, National Archives, Washington, DC.

Deeds, unrecorded. Camden County Historical Society. Camden, NJ.

Gloucester County, NJ. Boundaries of Land. Gloucester County Clerk's Office, Woodbury, NJ.

———. Court of Quarter Sessions and Common Pleas, Minutes. Gloucester County Historical Society, Woodbury, NJ.

———. Deed Books. Gloucester County Historical Society, Woodbury, NJ.

———. Land Division Books. Gloucester County Surrogate's Office, Woodbury, NJ.

———. Maps. Gloucester County Historical Society, Woodbury, NJ.

———. Mortgage Books. Gloucester County Historical Society, Woodbury, NJ.

———. Road Books. Gloucester County Historical Society, Woodbury, NJ.

Hessisches Staatsarchiv, Marburg, Germany.

Historic American Building Survey. Library of Congress, Washington, DC.

Howell Papers. University Archives & Special Collections, Rowan University, Campbell Library, Glassboro, NJ.

Lidgerwood Collection. Library, Morristown National Historical Park, Morristown, NJ.

Map Collection. Camden County Historical Society, Camden, NJ.

Maps of North America, 1750–1789. Library of Congress, Washington, DC.

New Jersey, State of. Archaeology Files. New Jersey Historic Preservation Office, Trenton.

———. Auditor's Account Book B. Department of the Treasury, State Treasurer's Office Records. New Jersey State Archives, Trenton.

———. Department of Defense, Adjutant General's Office (Revolutionary War) Records Including Numbered Manuscripts, Records of Commissioners of Forfeited Estates, 1777–1795, Revolutionary War Slips, and Revolutionary War Damage Claims. New Jersey State Archives, Trenton.

———. Liber AB of Commissions, Secretary of State's Office. New Jersey State Archives, Trenton.

———. National Register of Historic Places Files. New Jersey Historic Preservation Office, Trenton.

————. Ratable (Tax) Books (Duplicates), 1768–1846. General Assembly Records. New Jersey State Archives, Trenton.

————. Surveys and Warrants and Deed Books. Proprietors of West Jersey. New Jersey State Archives, Trenton.

————. Wills and Inventories. Secretary of State's Office Records. New Jersey State Archives, Trenton.

Photograph Collections. Gloucester City Historical Society, Gloucester City, NJ.

Queen, James Fuller. *House and Factories as Seen on the Edge of a Community.* Marian S. Carson Collection, Prints and Photographs Division, Library of Congress, Washington, DC.

Redman, Thomas. "The Journal of Thomas Redman." 1890 newspaper clipping. Gloucester County Historical Society, Woodbury, NJ.

Religious Society of Friends (Quakers). Most accessible at Ancestry. com, https://www.ancestry.com/search/collections/2189/.

————. "A Book Wherein Is Recorded the Births of Friends Children. . . ." Haddonfield Monthly Meeting [Ancestry listed as minutes, 1644–1845].

————. "Minutes of the Women Friends of the Monthly Meeting held at sundry Places as by Adjournments from the year 1705." Haddonfield Monthly Meeting [Ancestry listed as Haddonfield Monthly Meeting, Women's Minutes, 1705–1769].

————. Miscellaneous Papers. Philadelphia Meeting for Suffering. Friends Historical Library, Swarthmore College, Swarthmore, PA.

————. Monthly Meeting Minutes, vol. 2 (1731-1761). Haddonfield Monthly Meeting [Ancestry listed as minutes 1731–1935].

————. Monthly Meeting Minutes, vol. 3 (1762-1781) [Ancestry listed as minutes 1760–1781].

————. Salem [& Haddonfield] Quarterly Meeting Minutes, vol. 1 (1697–1776).

Sanborn Fire Insurance Maps. Library of Congress, Washington, DC.

————. Maps and Geospatial Data. Princeton University Library, Princeton.

Stewart, Frank H. Collection. University Archives & Special Collections, Rowan University, Campbell Library, Glassboro, NJ.

Tustin, Joseph P. Papers. Harvey A. Andruss Library Special Collections, Bloomsburg University, Bloomsburg, PA.

Washington, George. George Washington Papers. Library of Congress, Washington, DC.

PRIMARY SOURCES

Adams, John. *The Papers of John Adams*. Series 3: General and Public Correspondence, vol. 8 (March 1779–February 1780), edited by Gregg L. Lint et al. Cambridge, MA: Harvard University Press, 1989. Adams Papers Online.

Adams, John Quincy. *Memoirs of John Quincy Adams, Comprising Portions of His Diary from 1795 to 1848*. Edited by Charles Francis Adams. 12 vols. Philadelphia: J. B. Lippincott, 1874–77. Google Book.

André, John. *Major André's Journal*. Edited by Henry Cabot Lodge. Tarrytown, NY: William Abbatt, 1930.

Angell, Israel. The Diary of Colonel Israel Angell. MS transcribed and digitized by Norman Desmarais. Providence College digital archives. http://digitalcommons.providence.edu/primary/2/.

———. "The Israel Angell Diary, 1 October 1777–28 February 1778." Edited by Joseph Lee Boyle. *Rhode Island History* 58, no. 4 (2000): 107-138.

Archives of the State of New Jersey. *Documents Relating to the Colonial History of the State of New Jersey*. Archives of the State of New Jersey, 1st ser., 42 vols. NJ, various places: 1880–1949.

———. *Documents Relating to the Revolutionary History of the State of New Jersey*. Archives of the State of New Jersey, 2nd ser., 5 vols. Trenton: 1901–1917.

———. *New Jersey Archives*, 3rd ser., 5 vols. Trenton: New Jersey State Library, 1974–1986.

Auerbach, Inge, and Otto Fröhlich. *Hessische Truppen im Amerikanischen*. Vol. 4. Marburg, Germany: Archivschule Marburg, 1976. http://www.lagis-hessen.de/en/subjects/index/sn/hetrina.

Baurmeister, Carl Leopold. *Revolution in America: Confidential Letters and Journals 1776–1784 of Adjutant General Major Baurmeister of the Hessian Forces*. Translated and annotated by Bernard A. Uhlendorf. New Brunswick, NJ: Rutgers University Press, 1957.

Blodget, William. Major William Blodget to General George Weedon, November 25 [24], 1777. Gilder Lehrman Collection. https://www.gilderlehrman.org/collection/glc0649802.

Burgoyne, Bruce E., and Marie E. Burgoyne. *Journal of the Hesse-Cassel Jaeger Corps and Hans Konze's List of Jaeger Officers.* Westminster, MD: Heritage Books, 2008.

Burnett, Edmund C. *Letters of the Members of the Continental Congress.* 7 vols. Washington, DC: Carnegie Institute of Washington, 1921–1936. HathiTrust Digital Library, https://catalog.hathitrust.org/Record/001142323.

Cadwalader, John. *A Reply to General Joseph Reed's Remarks on a Late Publication in the Independent Gazetteer.* Philadelphia: T. Bradford, 1783. Reprint ca. 1847–48. HathiTrust Digital Library, https://catalog.hathitrust.org/Record/009587173.

Cattell, Jonas. "Reminiscences." *Woodbury* (NJ) *Constitution,* March 10, 1846.

Chastellux, François Jean de Beauvoir, marquis de. *Travels in North-America in the Years 1780–81–82.* 2 vols. London: Printed for G. G. J. and J. Robinson, 1787. HathiTrust Digital Library.

Clinton, Sir Henry. *The American Rebellion: Sir Henry Clinton's Narrative of his Campaigns, 1775–1782.* Edited by William B. Willcox. New Haven, CT: Yale University Press, 1954.

Continental Congress. *Journals of the Continental Congress, 1774–1789.* Edited by Worthington Chauncey Ford. Vol. 9, October 3–December 31, 1777. Washington, DC: Government Printing Office, 1907. HathiTrust Digital Library, https://catalog.hathitrust.org/Record/006538387.

———. *Letters of Delegates to Congress, 1774–1789.* Edited by Paul H. Smith. Vol. 8. Washington, DC: Library of Congress, 1981. American Memory, Library of Congress, http://memory.loc.gov/ammem/amlaw/lwdg.html.

Croker, John Wilson. *The Croker Papers: The Correspondence and Diaries of the Late Right Honourable John Wilson Croker, LL.D., F.R.S, Secretary of the Admiralty from 1809 to 1830.* Edited by Louis J. Jennings. 3 vols., 2nd ed. London: John Murray, 1885. Google Books.

Deane, Silas. *The Deane Papers, 1774–1790,* Collections of the New-York Historical Society for the Year 1886, vol. 1. New York: New-

York Historical Society, 1887. HathiTrust Digital Library, https://catalog.hathitrust.org/Record/002047621

Dearborn, Henry. *Revolutionary War Journals of Henry Dearborn*. Edited by Lloyd A. Brown and Howard H. Peckham. Chicago: Caxton Club, 1939.

Diderot, Dennis. *A Diderot Pictorial Encyclopedia of Trades and Industry*. Edited by Charles Coulston Gillispie. 2 vols. New York: Dover, 1959.

————. *Encyclopédie ou Dictionnaire raisonné des sciences, des arts et des métiers, par une Société de Gens de lettres*, vol. 4. Paris, 1754.

Doehlemann, Johann Christoph. "Diary of Johann Christoph Doehlemann, Grenadier Company, Ansbach Regiment, March 1777 to September 1778." Transcribed by Karl Walther. Translated by Henry J. Retzer. *The Hessians: Journal of the Johannes Schwalm Historical Association* 11 (2008): 11-17.

Döhla, Johann Conrad. *A Hessian Diary of the American Revolution*. Translated and edited by Bruce E. Burgoyne. Norman: University of Oklahoma Press, 1990.

Downman, Francis. *The Services of Lieut.-Colonel Francis Downman, R.A.* Edited by Colonel F. A. Whinyates. London: Royal Artillery Institution, 1898.

Ewald, Johann. *Diary of the American War: A Hessian Journal.* Translated and edited by Joseph P. Tustin. New Haven, CT: Yale University Press, 1979.

Fisher, Sarah Logan. "'A Diary of Trifling Occurrences,' Philadelphia, 1776–1778." Edited by Nicholas B. Wainwright. *Pennsylvania Magazine of History and Biography* 82, no. 4 (Oct. 1958): 411-465.

Fithian, Philip Vickers. *The Beloved Cohansie of Philip Vickers Fithian.* Edited by F. Alan Palmer. Bridgeton, NJ: Cumberland County Historical Society, 1990.

Ford, Worthington Chauncey. "The Defences of Philadelphia in 1777." *Pennsylvania Magazine of History and Biography* 18 (1894): 1-19, 163-184, 329-353, 463-495; vol. 19 (1895): 72-86, 234-250, 359-373, 481-506; vol. 20 (1896): 87-116, 213-247, 391-404, 520-551; continues vol. 21.

Franklin, Benjamin. *The Works of Benjamin Franklin, including the Private as well as the Official and Scientific Correspondence.* 12 vols. Edited by John Bigelow. New York: G.P. Putnam's Sons, 1904.

https://oll.libertyfund.org/title/franklin-the-works-of-benjamin-franklin-vol-viii-letters-and-misc-writings-1779-1781#lf1438-08_head_068.

Freyenhagen, Wilhelm Johann Ernst. "Journal of Ensign/Lt. Wilhelm Ernst Freyenhagen Jr., 1776–1778," part 2. Edited by Donald M. Londahl-Smidt. *The Hessians: Journal of the Johannes Schwalm Historical Association* 14 (2011): f63-77.

Greene, Christopher. "Orderly Book of Colonel Christopher Greene," New Jersey Society of Pennsylvania, *Year Book for 1928*, 46-52.

Greene, Nathaniel. *The Papers of General Nathanael Greene*. 13 vols. 1976–2015. Vol. 2. Edited by Richard K. Showman. Chapel Hill: University of North Carolina Press, 1980.

Greenman, Jeremiah. *Diary of a Common Soldier of the American Revolution, 1775–1783*. Edited by Robert C. Bray and Paul E. Bushnell. DeKalb: Northern Illinois University Press, 1978.

Hamilton, Alexander. *The Papers of Alexander Hamilton*. Edited by Harold C. Syrett et al. 27 vols. New York: Columbia University Press, 1961–87. *Founders Online*, National Archives.

Huntington, Joshua, and Jedehiah Huntington. *Huntington Papers: Correspondence of the Brothers Joshua and Jedediah Huntington during the Period of the American Revolution*. Hartford: Connecticut Historical Society, 1923.

Jäeger Corps. "Journal of the Field Jäeger Corps." Translated by Bruce E. Burgoyne. *The Hessians: Journal of the Johannes Schwalm Historical Association* 3, no. 3 (1987): 45-62.

Kemble, Stephen. *Journals of Lieut. Col. Stephen Kemble, 1773–1789; and British Army orders: Gen. Sir William Howe, 1775–1778; Gen. Sir Henry Clinton, 1778; and Gen. Daniel Jones, 1778*. Boston: Greg Press, 1972.

Knyphausen, Wilhelm von. Lieutenant General Wilhelm von Knyphausen to Landgraf Friedrich II, November 30, 1777. Lidgerwood Collection, Letter G, fiche no. 56: 122-133, Library, Morristown National Historical Park, Morristown, NJ.

Lafayette, Gilbert du Motier, Marquis de. *Lafayette in the Age of the American Revolution: Selected Letters and Papers, 1776–1790*. Edited by Stanley J. Idzerda. Ithaca, NY: Cornell University Press, 1977–.

————. to Colonel Richard Butler, November 29, 1777. *Pennsylvania Magazine of History and Biography* 14 (1890): 83.

Lesser, Charles H., ed. *The Sinews of Independence: Monthly Strength Reports of the Continental Army.* Chicago: University of Chicago Press, 1976.

Livingston, William. *The Papers of William Livingston.* Edited by Carl E. Prince and Dennis P. Ryan. 5 vols. Trenton: New Jersey Historical Commission, 1979–1988.

Londahl-Smidt, Donald M. "German and British Accounts of the Assault on Fort Mercer at Redbank, NJ in October 1777." *The Hessians: Journal of the Johannes Schwalm Historical Association* 16 (2013): 1-33.

Montrésor, John. *The Montrésor Journals. Collections of the New York Historical Society for the Year 1882.* Edited by G. D. Scull. New York: New-York Historical Society, 1882.

Moraley, William. *The Infortunate: or, the Voyage and Adventures of William Moraley.* Edited by Susan E. Klepp and Billy G. Smith. University Park: Pennsylvania State University Press, 1992.

Morton, Robert. "The Diary of Robert Morton." *Pennsylvania Magazine of History and Biography* 1, no. 1 (1877): 1-39.

Muenchhausen, Friedrich von. *At General Howe's Side, 1776–1778.* Translated by Ernst Kipping. Edited by Samuel Stelle Smith. Monmouth Beach, NJ: Philip Freneau Press, 1974.

Naval History and Heritage Command. *Naval Documents of the American Revolution.* Edited by William James Morgan et al. Washington, DC: Department of the Navy, 1964– (13 vols. to date).

Newcomb, Silas. "Regimental Returns and Brigade Orders." *Proceedings of the New Jersey Historical Society,* ser. 2, no. 1 (1869): 37-40.

New Jersey, State of. *Acts of the Council and General Assembly of the State of New-Jersey from the Establishment of the present Government . . . to 24th Day of December, 1783.* Trenton: Isaac Collins, 1784. HathiTrust Digital Library, https://catalog.hathitrust.org/Record/010476368.

————. *Acts of the General Assembly of the Province of New-Jersey . . .* (1702–1776). Edited by Samuel Allinson. Burlington, NJ: Isaac Collins, 1776. HathiTrust.org, https://catalog.hathitrust.org/Record/010448351.

————. *Acts of the General Assembly of the State of New-Jersey . . . begun . . . 27th Day of August 1776.* Burlington, NJ: Isaac Collins, 1777–1778.

————. *Acts of the General Assembly of the State of New-Jersey . . . begun . . . 27th Day of October 1778.* Trenton: Isaac Collins, 1779.

————. *Acts of the Sixth General Assembly of the State of New-Jersey at a Session begun . . . 23d Day of October, 1781.* Trenton: Isaac Collins, 1782.

————. *Journal of the Proceedings of the Legislative-Council.* Burlington, NJ: Isaac Collins, 1777.

————. *Minutes and Proceedings of the Council and General Assembly of the State of New-Jersey in Joint-Meeting from August 30, 1777, to May, 1780.* Trenton: Isaac Collins, 1780.

————. *Minutes of the Council of Safety of the State of New Jersey.* Jersey City, NJ: John H. Lyon, 1872. HathiTrust Digital Library, https://catalog.hathitrust.org/api/volumes/oclc/2334867.html.

————. *Minutes of the Provincial Congress and the Council of Safety of the State of New Jersey.* Trenton: Naar, Day & Naar, 1879. Archives.org, https://archive.org/details/minutesofprovinc00newj.

————. *Votes and Proceedings of the General Assembly of the Province of New Jersey . . . begun March 11, 1760.* Woodbridge, NJ: James Parker, 1760.

————. *Votes and Proceedings of the General Assembly of the State of New Jersey . . . begun 27 August 1776.* Burlington, NJ: Isaac Collins, 1777.

————. *Votes and Proceedings of the Fifth General Assembly of the State of New-Jersey.* Trenton: Isaac Collins, 1780.

————. *Votes and Proceedings of the Twenty-Second General Assembly of the State of New-Jersey at a Session Begun . . . the Twenty-Fourth Day of October, Seventeen Hundred and Ninety-Seven.* Trenton: Matthias Day, 1797. NJStateLib.org., http://hdl.handle.net/10929/15117.

Pattison, James. *The James Pattison Papers, 1777–1781.* Edited by I. F. Burton. London: Royal Artillery Institution, 1963.

Peebles, John. *John Peebles' American War: The Diary of a Scottish Grenadier, 1776–1782.* Edited by Ira D. Gruber. Mechanicsburg, PA: Stackpole, 1998.

Pennsylvania, State of. *Minutes of the Provincial Council of Pennsylvania,* vol. 10 of the *Colonial Records of Pennsylvania* (Harrisburg: Theo.

Fenn, 1852), HathiTrust Digital Library, https://catalog.hathi trust.org/Record/000540855.

———. *Minutes of the Supreme Executive Council of Pennsylvania*, vol. 11 of the *Colonial Records of Pennsylvania*. Harrisburg: Theo. Fenn, 1852, HathiTrust Digital Library, https://catalog.hathitrust.org/Record/000540855.

———. *Original Documents in the Office of the Secretary of the Commonwealth, Commencing 1760*. Pennsylvania Archives, 1st ser., vol. 4. Philadelphia: Joseph Severns, 1853. Ancestry.com, https://www.ancestry.com/search/collections/2206/.

———. *Original Documents in the Office of the Secretary of the Commonwealth, Commencing 1776*. Pennsylvania Archives, 1st ser., vol. 5. Philadelphia: Joseph Severns, 1853. Ancestry.com, https://www.ancestry.com/search/collections/2206/.

———. *Original Documents in the Office of the Secretary of the Commonwealth, Commencing 1777*. Pennsylvania Archives, 1st ser., vol. 6. Philadelphia: Joseph Severns, 1853. Ancestry.com, https://www.ancestry.com/search/collections/2206/.

Popp, Stephan. *A Hessian Soldier in the American Revolution.* Translated by Reinhart J. Pope. Privately printed, 1953.

Prechtel, Johann Ernst. *A Hessian Officer's Diary.* Translated by Bruce E. Burgoyne. Westminster, MD: Heritage Books, 1994.

Redman, Thomas. "Thomas Redman's Account of His Being Apprehended & Imprisoned in the Common Goal at Gloucester." MS, Friends Historical Library, Swarthmore College, Swarthmore, PA.

Robertson, Archibald. *Archibald Robertson: His Diaries and Sketches in America, 1762–1780.* Edited by Harry Miller Lydenberg. New York: New York Public Library, 1930.

Serle, Ambrose. *The Journal of Ambrose Serle, Secretary to Lord Howe.* Edited by Edward H. Tatam Jr. San Marino, CA: Huntington Library, 1940.

Simcoe, John Graves. *Simcoe's Military Journal: A History of the Operations of the Queen's Rangers.* New York: Bartlett & Welford, 1844.

Smith, John. "'Thro Mud & Mire into the Woods': The 1777 Continental Army Diary of Sergeant John Smith, First Rhode

Island Regiment." Edited by Bob McDonald. http://www.rev war75.com/library/bob/smith.htm.

Steelman, Zephaniah. Report of Captain Steelman's Company . . . 9 Oct 1778. Col. Richard Somers' Papers. Digital Library @ Villanova University, https://library.villanova.edu/Find/Record/vudl:262293.

Stevens, Benjamin Franklin. *B. F. Stevens's Facsimiles of Manuscripts in European Archives Relating to America, 1773–1783.* London: Malby & Sons, 1889. HathiTrust Digital Library, https://catalog.hathi trust.org/Record/101739764,

Stirke, Henry [Julius]. "A British Officer's Revolutionary War Journal." Edited by S. Sydney Bradford. *Maryland Historical Magazine* 54 (1961): 150-175. While published as the journal of Lieutenant Henry Stirke, it is the journal of his brother, Captain Julius Stirke.

Stryker-Rodda, Kenn. "New Jersey Rateables, 1773–1774, Gloucester County." *Genealogical Magazine of New Jersey* 39, no. 1 (Jan. 1964): 8-16.

Wagner, Adjutant Johann Emanuel. Journal of Colonel von Donop, December 10–31, 1776. Lingerwood Collection, Morristown National Historical Park. Microfiche, letter C, 1- Boston: G. K. Hall, 1989.

Washington, George. Papers: Series 4. Manuscript Division, Library of Congress, Washington, DC.

———. *The Papers of George Washington: Presidential Series*, vol. 10. Edited by Philander D. Chase. Charlottesville: University Press of Virginia, 2002.

———. *The Papers of George Washington: Revolutionary War Series*, 29 vols. to date. Edited by Philander D. Chase. Charlottesville: University Press of Virginia, 1985–.

———. *The Writings of George Washington*, 39 vols. Edited by John C. Fitzpatrick. Washington, DC: Government Printing Office, 1931–1944.

Whitall, Job. *The Diary of Job Whitall of Gloucester County, New Jersey: 1775–1779.* Transcribed by Florence DeHuff Friel. Woodbury, NJ: Gloucester County Historical Society, 1992.

Wilkinson, James. *Memoirs of My Own Times.* 3 vols. Philadelphia: Abraham Small, 1816. HathiTrust Digital Library, https://catalog. hathitrust.org/Record/000877719.

Wilson, Thomas B., comp. "Records of John Stevens Regarding the New Jersey Regiment in the French & Indian War." Unpublished manuscript, New Jersey State Archives, Trenton.

MAPS

Anonymous. Manuscript map of eastern Pennsylvania from the Delaware to the Susquehanna. Clinton map 250. Clements Library, University of Michigan, Ann Arbor.

———. *Map of British Outposts between Burlington and New Bridge, New Jersey, December [1776]*. Library of Congress (ct000077).

———. *Map of the Coast of New Jersey from Barnegat Inlet to Cape May.* Library of Congress (ct000078).

———. *Plan and Sections of the Redoubt at Billingsfort and Plan of the Rebel Fort Marked Yellow.* Library of Congress (ar127600).

———. *Red Banke.* Library of Congress (ar127500). [A 1777 beautifully rendered map inaccurately drawn from memory. Valuable for two, dimensioned cross sections of the fortifications apparently measured by a British engineer prior to the fort's demolition in November 1777.]

[Cadwalader, John]. *Draft of Roads in New Jersey* [Detailed sketch map of western Gloucester County, circa November 1777]. Library of Congress (ar126300).

Chesnoy, Michel Capitaine du. *Carte de l'action de Gloucester entre un parti Americain d'environ 350 hommes sous le Gl Lafayette et un parti des Troupes de Lord Cornowalis, commande par ce Gl apres son fourage dans le Jersay le 25 9bre 1777.* Cornell University Library, Division of Rare and Manuscript Collections, G3701.S323P4 1777 C3 mapcase.

———. *Carte des positions occupeés par les trouppes Américaines apres leur retraite de Rhode Island le 30 Aout 1778.* Library of Congress (ar300400).

———. *Plan de la retraite de Barren Hill en Pensilvanie: ou un détachement de deux mille deux cent hommes sous le G'al LaFayette étois entouré par l'Armée angloise . . .* Library of Congress (ar300100).

———. *Plan de Rhode Islande, les differentes operations de la flotte françoise et des trouppes Américaines commandeés par le major général Sullivan contre les forces de terre et de mer des Anglois depuis le 9 Aout jusqu'a la nuit du 30 au 31 du même mois que les Américains ont fait leur retraite 1778.* Library of Congress (ar300300).

Clement, John. Maps and Drafts, 7 vols. (1845–1881). Clement Papers. Historical Society of Pennsylvania, Philadelphia.

Cook, George H., and C. C. Vermeule. *A Topographic Survey of the Vicinity of Camden to Burlington, Winslow, Elmer and Swedesboro.* Geological Survey of New Jersey, atlas sheet 11. Trenton: Geological Survey of New Jersey, 1888. New York University Spatial Data Repository.

Erskine, Robert, et al. New-York Historical Society. No. 87E: *Road from upper end of Kingsington to Market House in Philadelphia, and from thence two others, vizt.; from Market House to Falls of Schuylkill and from Cooper's Ferry past the 14 M. S. from Burlington.*

———. No. 87F: *Road from near the 14 MS. from Burlington thro Moorstown & to one James Sippingwills.*

———. No. 124A: *From Philadelphia through Darby + Chester to the Anchor Tavern.*

Ewald, Johann. *Plan, von dem Angriff aufs Fort bei Read Bank.* Bloomsburg University, Harvey A. Andruss Library, Bloomsburg, PA. https://library.bloomu.edu/Archives/Maps/map101.htm.

Hills, John. *A Plan of Philadelphia and Environs.* Philadelphia: John Hills, 1808, with revisions. Princeton University.

———. *A Sketch of Haddonfield, West New Jersey County.* Henry Clinton Papers, Brun Guide 584. William L. Clements Library, Ann Arbor, MI.

Hopkins, G. M. *Atlas of Philadelphia and Environs.* Philadelphia: G. M. Hopkins, 1877. Map Division, Free Library of Philadelphia.

———. *Map of the City of Gloucester, New Jersey.* Philadelphia: G. M. Hopkins, 1877. Camden County Historical Society.

New Jersey. *Aerial Atlas 1930.* Georeferenced by Craig Coutros. New Jersey Department of Environmental Protection, Bureau of Geographic Information Systems, Trenton.

Nicole, Pierre. *Plan of the City of Philadelphia and Its Environs Shewing Its Defences during the Years 1777 & 1778, together with the Siege of Mud Island.* Library of Congress (ar132400).

———. *A Survey of the City of Philadelphia and Its Environs Shewing the Several Works Constructed by His Majesty's Troops . . . Likewise the Attacks against Fort Mifflin.* Library of Congress (ar302200).

United States Department of Agriculture and the New Jersey Geological Survey. *Soil Map, New Jersey, Camden Sheet.* Baltimore: A. Hoen, 1915. http://alabamamaps.ua.edu/historicalmaps/soilsurvey /New%20Jersey/new%20jersey.html.

Wangenheim, Friedrich Adam Julius von. *Les marches du corps du Lord Cornwallis de Billingsport jusqu'a Philadelphia au mois de Novembre, 1777.* Library of Congress (ar127700).

NEWSPAPERS (ACCESSED THROUGH NEWSPAPERS.COM)

Dunlap's Pennsylvania Packet (Lancaster)
Dunlap's Pennsylvania Packet (Philadelphia)
Independent Gazetteer (Philadelphia)
Jackson's Oxford Journal (UK)
Maryland Gazette (Annapolis)
Pennsylvania Gazette (Philadelphia)
Purdie's *Virginia Gazette* (Williamsburg)
Virginia Gazette (Williamsburg)

SECONDARY SOURCES

Armstrong, William C. *Pioneer Settlers of Northeastern New Jersey.* Lambertville, NJ: Hunterdon House, 1979.

Boyer, Charles S. "Appendix." In Carlos E. Godfrey, "The True Origin of Old Gloucester County, N.J.: A paper read before the Camden County Historical Society 21 November 1922." *Camden History* 1, no. 4.

———. *Old Ferries, Camden, New Jersey.* Annals of Camden no. 3. Privately printed, 1921.

———. *Old Inns and Taverns in West Jersey.* Camden, NJ: Camden County Historical Society, 1962.

———. *Old Mills of Camden County.* Camden, NJ: Camden County Historical Society, 1962.

Burke, R. T. Avon, and L. L. Lee. *Soil Survey of the Camden Area, New Jersey.* Washington, DC: US Department of Agriculture, 1926.

Cloquet, Jules Germain. *Recollections of the Private Life of General Lafayette.* 2 vols. New York: Leavitt, Lord, 1836.

Coleman, Mary Haldane Begg. *St. George Tucker: Citizen of No Mean City.* Richmond, VA: Dietz Press, 1938. Internet Archive, https://archive.org/details/stgeorgetuckerci00cole.

Commonwealth Heritage Group. "'It is Painful for Me to Lose so Many Good People': Report of an Archeological Survey at Red Bank Battlefield Park." West Chester, PA: 2017. Unpublished manuscript prepared for the American Battlefield Protection Program, Grant GA-2287-004.

Crauderueff, Elaine J. *War Taxes: Experiences of Philadelphia Yearly Meeting Quakers through the American Revolution.* Wallingford, PA: Pendle Hill, 1989.

Crumrine, Boyd, ed. *History of Washington County, Pennsylvania.* Philadelphia: L. H. Everts, 1882.

Cushing, Thomas, and Charles E. Sheppard. *History of the Counties of Gloucester, Salem, and Cumberland, New Jersey.* Philadelphia: Everts & Peck, 1883.

Dann, John C. *The Revolution Remembered: Eyewitness Accounts of the War for Independence.* Chicago: University of Chicago Press, 1980.

DeCou, George. *Moorestown and Her Neighbors.* 3rd ed. Moorestown, NJ: Moorestown Historical Society, 1982.

Duncan, Mike. *Hero of Two Worlds: The Marquis de Lafayette in the Age of Revolution.* New York: PublicAffairs, 2021.

Dwyer, William M. *The Day Is Ours!* New York: Viking, 1983.

Farr, William R. *Watermills of Camden County.* http://www.westjersey history.org/books/farrwatermills/E.shtml.

———. *Waterways of Camden County: A Historical Gazetteer.* Camden, NJ: Camden County Historical Society, 2002.

Fischer, David Hackett. *Washington's Crossing.* New York: Oxford University Press, 2004.

Founders Online. "A Sword for the Marquis de Lafayette." https://founders.archives.gov/documents/Franklin/01-30-02-0203.

Gilbert, Stephen. "Grenadier Glory and Missed Chances: New Jersey, Pennsylvania, New Jersey & New York, 23 March 1777–2 November 1778." Chap. 12 in "British Grenadiers." Unpublished manuscript, last modified 2005.

———. "Light Infantry in New Jersey, Pennsylvania, and New York, 1777–1778." Chap. 3 in "British Light Infantry." Unpublished manuscript, last modified March 2020.

Gottschalk, Louis. *Lafayette and the Close of the American Revolution.* Chicago: University of Chicago Press, 1942, 1965.

————. *Lafayette Comes to America*. Chicago: University of Chicago Press, 1935.

————. *Lafayette Joins the American Army*. Chicago: University of Chicago Press, 1965.

Graham, James. *The Life of General Daniel Morgan*. New York: Derby & Jackson, 1859.

Gruber, Ira D. *The Howe Brothers and the American Revolution*. Chapel Hill: University of North Carolina Press, 1972.

Guthorn, Peter J. *American Maps and Map Makers of the Revolution*. Monmouth Beach, NJ: Philip Freneau Press, 1966.

————. *British Maps of the American Revolution*. Monmouth Beach, NJ: Philip Freneau Press, 1972.

Harvey, Oscar Jewell, and Ernest Gray Smith. *A History of Wilkes-Barré, Luzerne County, Pennsylvania*. 6 vols. Wilkes-Barré, PA: Raeder Press, 1909–1930. HathiTrust Digital Library, https://catalog.hathitrust.org/Record/012262872.

Heitman, Francis B. *Historical Register of Officers of the Continental Army during the War of the Revolution, April 1775, to December, 1783*. Washington, DC: Rare Book Shop Publishing, 1914. Reprint, Baltimore: Genealogical Publishing, 1982.

Higginbotham, Don. *Daniel Morgan: Revolutionary Rifleman*. Chapel Hill: University of North Carolina Press, 1979.

Hodapp, Christopher. *Solomon's Builders: Freemasons, Founding Fathers and the Secrets of Washington, D.C.* Berkeley, CA: Ulysses Press, 2007.

Honors History 12. *Driving Tour of the Battle of Whitemarsh*. Edited by Thomas Sorkness. Erdenheim, PA: Philadelphia-Montgomery Christian Academy, 2017. https://battleofwhitemarsh.weebly.com/.

Jackson, John W. *The Pennsylvania Navy, 1775–1781: The Defense of the Delaware*. New Brunswick, NJ: Rutgers University Press, 1965.

————. *With the British Army in Philadelphia, 1777–1778*. San Rafael, CA: Presidio Press, 1979.

Ketchum, Richard M. *Saratoga*. New York: Henry Holt, 1997.

Kiddoo, Donald B. "Major Joseph Morris in Action." Veterans Day tribute presented by the First Presbyterian Church, Whippany, NJ. Copy at North Jersey History Center, Morristown and Morris Township Library.

Kite, Elizabeth S. "Lafayette and His Companions on the 'Victoire.'" *Records of the American Catholic Society* 45, no. 1 (March 1934): 1-32. JSTOR.org., https://www.jstor.org/stable/44209160?refreqid= excelsior%3A697a62fde96fec7aad8867602fd07f6e.

LaCrosse, Richard B., Jr. *Revolutionary Rangers.* Westminster, MD: Heritage Books, 2007.

Lefkowitz, Arthur S. *The Long Retreat: The Calamitous American Defense of New Jersey, 1776.* Metuchen, NJ: Upland Press, 1998.

Lender, Mark Edward. *Cabal! The Plot against General Washington.* Yardley, PA: Westholme, 2019.

Lender, Mark Edward, and Garry Wheeler Stone. *Fatal Sunday: George Washington, the Monmouth Campaign, and the Politics of Battle.* Norman: University of Oklahoma Press, 2016.

Lesser, Charles H., ed. *The Sinews of Independence: Monthly Strength Reports of the Continental Army.* Chicago: University of Chicago Press, 1976.

Levasseur, Auguste. *Lafayette in America in 1824 and 1825.* 2 vols. Translated by John D. Godman. Philadelphia: Carey and Lea, 1829. Google Book.

Louis Berger & Associates, Inc. "Survey and Evaluation of Historical and Archaeological Resources at the Former United States Coast Guard Station, City of Gloucester, Camden County, New Jersey." East Orange, NJ, July 1994. Unpublished manuscript on file at the New Jersey Historic Preservation Office, Trenton, NJ.

MAAR Associates. "Data Recovery at 28Ca50, Gloucester City, New Jersey." 3 vols. Newark, DE, 1984. Unpublished manuscript on file at the NJ Historic Preservation Office, Trenton, NJ.

McBurney, Christian M. "Presentation Swords for 10 Revolutionary War Heroes." *Journal of the American Revolution* May 16, 2014. https://allthingsliberty.com/2014/05/presentation-swords-for-ten-revolutionary-war-heroes.

McCusker, John J. "How Much Is That in Real Money? A Historical Price Index." *Proceedings of the American Antiquarian Society* 101, part 2 (Oct 1991): 297-373.

McGuire, Thomas J. *The Philadelphia Campaign: Volume 1, Brandywine and the Fall of Philadelphia.* Mechanicsburg, PA: Stackpole 2006.

————. *The Philadelphia Campaign: Volume 2, Germantown and the Roads to Valley Forge*. Mechanicsburg, PA: Stackpole 2007.

Milnor, William. *An Authentic Historical Memoir of the Schuylkill Fishing Company of the State of Schuylkill . . . with Memoirs of the Gloucester Fox Hunting Club*. Philadelphia: Judah Dobson, 1830. Archive.org., https://archive.org/details/authentichistori00miln.

Morrissey, Brendan. *Saratoga 1777*. Oxford, UK: Osprey, 2000.

Mount Ephraim Bicentennial Committee. *A History of Mount Ephraim*. Mount Ephraim, NJ: Bicentennial Committee, 1976.

Mowday, Bruce E. *Lafayette at Brandywine: The Making of an American Hero*. Fort Lee, NJ: Barricade Books, 2021.

Munn, David C. "A Visit to Gloucester Town." Unpublished manuscript in the possession of the authors.

Nelson, William. *New Jersey Biographical and Genealogical Notes from the Volumes of the New Jersey Archives*. Newark: New Jersey Historical Society, 1916.

Nolan, J. Bennett. *Lafayette in America Day by Day*. Baltimore: Johns Hopkins University Press, 1934. HathiTrust Digital Library, https://catalog.hathitrust.org/Record/001655979.

Outland, Ruth M. "A History of Haddonfield Friends' School." MA thesis, Columbia University, 1938.

Patrick, A. L., C. C. Engle, and L. L. Lee. *Soil Survey of the Camden Area, New Jersey*. Washington, DC: Government Printing Office, 1917.

Peterson, Charles E. *Robert Smith: Architect, Builder, Patriot, 1722–1777*. Philadelphia: The Athenæum of Philadelphia, 2000.

Pichichero, Christy L. *The Military Enlightenment: War and Culture in the French Empire from Louis XIV to Napoleon*. Ithaca, NY: Cornell University Press, 2017.

Pierce, Arthur D. *Iron in the Pines*. New Brunswick, NJ: Rutgers University Press, 1957.

Prowell, George R. *History of Camden County, New Jersey*. Philadelphia: L. J. Richards, 1886. HathiTrust Digital Library, https://catalog.hathitrust.org/Record/009601482.

Richard Grubb & Associates. "Supplemental Phase I/Phase II Archaeological Survey and Terminal Phase II Archaeological Survey, 28-CA-128, -129, -130, -131, -132, Gloucester City Elementary/Middle School, Gloucester City, Camden, NJ."

Unpublished manuscript, New Jersey Historic Preservation Office Project #05-2020. Cranbury, NJ, 2015.

Richman, Steven M. "The Battle of Millstone." *Journal of the American Revolution*, October 22, 2014. https://allthingsliberty.com/2014/10/the-battle-of-millstone.

Schopp, Paul W. "Historic Cultural Context." New Jersey Department of Transportation, I-295/I-76/Route 42 Direct Connection, Phase I/II Archaeological Investigation Technical Environmental. Vol. 1, March 2006. http://www.state.nj.us/transportation/commuter/roads/rt295/pdf/PhaseI-IIArchaeoInvest TESVol_I.pdf.

———. "The Hugg/Harrison/Glover House (New Saint Mary's Cemetery), Borough of Bellmawr, Camden County, New Jersey." *History—Now and Then* (blog). http://jerseyman-historynowand then.blogspot.com/2010/09/huggharrisonglover-house-new-st-marys.html.

———. "The Plantation Yclept Bromley." *History—Now and Then* (blog). http://jerseyman-historynowandthen.blogspot.com/2010/11/plantation-yclept-bromley.html.

Selig, Robert A. "African-Americans, the Rhode Island Regiments, and the Battle of Fort Red Bank, 22 October 1777." Unpublished manuscript prepared for Gloucester County, NJ, 2019.

Shinn, Robert, Andrew Levecchia, and Sandra White Grear. "The Newton Union Burial Ground." *SoJourn* (Winter 2018/19).

Shomette, Donald Grady. *Privateers of the Revolution: War on the New Jersey Coast, 1775–1783.* Atglen, PA: Schiffer, 2016.

Smith, Horace Wemyss. *Life and Correspondence of the Rev. William Smith, D.D.* 2 vols. Philadelphia: Ferguson Bros., 1880. HathiTrust Digital Library, https://catalog.hathitrust.org/Record/008640135.

Spees, Everett K. "Hessen-Cassel Erbprinz Fusilier Regiment Prepares and Departs of America—1776." *The Hessians* 22 (2019): 16-37.

Stewart, Frank H. *History of the Battle of Red Bank with Events Prior and Subsequent Thereto.* Woodbury, NJ: Gloucester County Freeholders, 1927.

———. *Notes on Old Gloucester County.* Vol. 1. Camden, NJ: Sinnickson Chew & Sons, 1917.

———. *Notes on Old Gloucester County.* Vol. 2. Woodbury, NJ: The Constitution, 1933.

———. *Notes on Old Gloucester County.* Vol. 3. Woodbury, NJ: The Constitution, 1937.

Stone, Edwin Martin. "The Invasion of Canada in 1775: Including the Journal of Captain Simeon Thayer, with Notes and Appendix." *Collections of the Rhode Island Historical Society* 6 (1867): 1-105.

Stone, Garry Wheeler. "Coopers Ferry, New Jersey, during the American Revolution." Report to the American Battlefield Protection Program, NPS, September 28, 2015. Copy on file with the Camden County Historical Society, Camden, NJ.

———. "The Whitall Family of Red Bank and Woodbury during the American Revolution, 1775–1779: The Plight of Quaker Pacifists in a War Zone." Report to the American Battlefield Protection Program, NPS, September 28, 2015. *Bulletin of the Gloucester County Historical Society* 36, no. 4 (Summer 2018): 31, 33-36.

Stone, Garry Wheeler, and Paul W. Schopp. "Bellmawr in the American Revolution." *Bulletin of the Gloucester County Historical Society* 35, no. 7 (March 2017): 59, 61-66.

———. "Gloucester, New Jersey: A Forgotten Battle of the American Revolution." Report to the American Battlefield Protection Program, NPS, September 2019. Copy on file with the Camden County Historical Society, Camden, NJ.

Störkel, Arno. "The Ansback Jägers." *The Hessians* 14 (2011): 1-31.

Stryker, William Scudder, comp. *Official Register of the Officers and Men of New Jersey in the Revolutionary War.* Trenton: Wm. T. Nicholson, 1872.

Thayer, Theodore. *Nathanael Greene, Strategist of the American Revolution.* New York: Twayne Publishers, 1960.

Thibaut, Jacqueline. *This Fatal Crisis: Logistics and the Continental Army at Valley Forge, 1777–1778.* Vol. 2 of *The Valley Forge Historical Research Report.* Valley Forge, PA: Valley Forge National Historical Park, 1982.

Thomas, Ronald A., and Martha J. Schiek. "Excavations at a late 17th-Century House Site in Gloucester City, New Jersey." Unpublished manuscript submitted to the National Park Service, 1985. Newark, DE, MAAR Associates. New Jersey Historic Preservation Office, CAM H92 vol.1.

Thomas, Ronald A., Martha J. Schiek et al. "Archaeological Data Recovery at 28 CA 50, Gloucester City, New Jersey." Report submitted to the National Park Service, April 1985. Newark, DE, MAAR Associates. New Jersey Historic Preservation Office, CAM H92 vol.2.

Tower, Champagne. *The Marquis de Lafayette in the American Revolution.* 2nd ed. 2 vols. Philadelphia: J. B. Lippincott, 1901. HathiTrust Digital Library, https://catalog.hathitrust.org/Record/006785134.

Unger, Harlow Giles. *Lafayette.* Hoboken, NJ: John Wiley & Sons, 2002.

United States Department of Agriculture. *Soil Survey of the Camden Area, New Jersey.* Washington, DC: Government Printing Office, 1917.

Valis, Glen, and Georgeanne Valis. "The Battle of Millstone." New Jersey during the Revolution. Accessed March 7, 2020. http://www.doublegv.com/ggv/battles/millstone.html.

Wacker, Peter O., and Paul G. E. Clements. *Land Use in Early New Jersey.* Newark: New Jersey Historical Society, 1995.

Ward, Harry M. *Major General Adam Stephen and the Cause of American Liberty.* Charlottesville: University Press of Virginia, 1989.

———. *When Fate Summons: A Biography of General Richard Butler, 1743–1791.* Palo Alto, CA: Academica Press, 2014.

Winfield, Rif. *British Warships in the Age of Sail, 1714–1792.* Barnsley, UK: Seaforth, 2007.

Zucker, Adolf Eduard. *General de Kalb, Lafayette's Mentor.* Chapel Hill: University of North Carolina Press, 1966.

INTERNET LIBRARIES

We found the following internet sites helpful, especially during the COVID-19 pandemic when we were not able to visit libraries. Some of these sites are free. Others require subscriptions.

Ancestry. https://www.ancestry.com. (Access to battlefield family genealogies and *Archives of the State of New Jersey, Colonial Records of Pennsylvania,* and *Pennsylvania Archives.*)

Fold3 by Ancestry. https://www.fold3.com/. (Records of the Continental army, including army, regimental, and individual soldier files. Some names linked to the papers of the Continental Congress. Not user friendly but invaluable.)

Google Books. https://books.google.com.

HathiTrust Digital Library. www.hathitrust.org. (Millions of publications.)

Internet Archive. https://archive.org. (Nonprofit library of millions of free books, movies, software, music, websites, and more.)

JSTOR. https://www.jstor.org. (Digital library of academic journals, books, and primary sources.)

Library of Congress. "American Revolution and Its Era: Maps and Charts of North America and the West Indies, 1750 to 1789." https://www.loc.gov/collections/american-revolutionary-war-maps.

National Archives. Founders Online. https://founders.archives.gov. (Correspondence and other writings of seven major shapers of the United States: George Washington, Benjamin Franklin, John Adams, Thomas Jefferson, Alexander Hamilton, John Jay, and James Madison.)

New Jersey State Archives. https://www.nj.gov/state/archives/index.html. (Several searchable databases including land records.)

New Jersey State Library. https://www.njstatelib.org/research_library/legal_resources/historical_laws/legislative_journals_and_minutes/. (Legislation and proceedings of the New Jersey State Assembly and Council.)

Newspapers.Com by Ancestry. https://www.newspapers.com/. (Political news, advertisements.)

New-York Historical Society Digital Collections, https://digitalcollections.nyhistory.org/islandora/object/islandora%3Amaps. (Robert Erskine and Simeon DeWitt military maps, 1778-1783.)

Royal Provincial.com. http://www.royalprovincial.com. (On-line Institute for Advanced Loyalist Studies [Todd Braisted].)

Southern Campaign Pensions and Rosters. https://revwarapps.org/.

West Jersey History Project. http://www.westjerseyhistory.org/.

Wikipedia. https://www.wikipedia.org/.

Acknowledgments

THE AUTHORS ARE PROFOUNDLY GRATEFUL to the compilers, translators, and editors who have assembled and published the abundance of Revolutionary War papers that made this book possible. We are especially grateful to the individuals who made the German records accessible, particularly Bruce E. Burgoyne and Colonel Donald M. Londahl-Smidt. Jason R. Wickersty provided transcriptions of all the skirmish mentions found in the pension applications of New Jersey soldiers. Stephen Gilbert provided the names of the two British light infantrymen killed during the skirmish at the Big Timber Creek bridge, Eric Stephenson provided the photograph of David Mulford's memorial, and William T. Lawrence translated the Capitaine map legend. Librarians Kathie Ludwig (David Library of the American Revolution) and Bonny Beth Elwell (Camden County Historical Society) assisted us in our research. At Lafayette College, Pamela Murray arranged for scans of Dr. Jules Germain Cloquet's drawings of Lafayette's sword. In Woodbury, Barbara Price guided us through the wealth of county documents at the Gloucester County Historical Society, and, across the street at the Gloucester County surrogate's office, the staff allowed us to photograph portions of the land division books. At the New Jersey State Archives, Bette Epstein provided exceptional service, and Executive Director Joseph R. Klett furnished copies of the Galloway Township and Great Egg Harbor tax lists. At Rowan University's Campbell Library, Sara Borden provided access to the militia court-martial papers in the Stewart Collection. Glenn Campbell, Historic Annapolis, provided information on Edmund Brice (he is preparing an article on the Brice brothers). Brad J. Hafner, of the New Jersey Department of Transportation Engineering Documents Unit, provided us with the 1957 Interstate 295 construction drawings for the site of the Harrison-Eldridge-Glover gristmill. We would have found ourselves lost among Camden County's early roads except for Edward Fox's meticulous mapping of road returns—mapping conveniently provided as an ArcMap feature dataset.

Members of the Haddon Heights Historical Society—Bob Hunter, Elena Hill, Rosemary Fitzgerald, and Margaret Westfield—provided research materials on the Thorne-Glover House and Haddon Lake Park. Cherilyn Widell, Historical Society of Haddonfield, provided a copy of Ruth Outland's thesis on the Haddonfield Friends' School. Gloucester City Historical Society member Patrick Ward served almost as a part of the research team, providing scans of historic photographs and maps, and locating two additional versions of the Capitaine map. Ward also assisted Camden County Historical Society staff member Joshua Lisowski in transporting two historic maps to the Philadelphia Athenaeum. There, Michael Seneca, director of the Digital Imaging Center, facilitated the scanning of the maps. Members of BRAVO, the Battlefield Restoration and Archaeological Volunteer Organization, provided the ArcMap software used in producing the maps.

A residential fellowship at the David Library provided Garry Stone the opportunity to conduct research for the military history portion of this report. Two grants from the American Battlefield Protection Program, National Park Service, subsidized our research into the battlefield's cultural history. Both grants sought to increase public awareness of the Revolutionary War history and historic sites within Old Gloucester County. Grant GA-2287-13-

011, to the Friends of the Indian King Tavern Museum, focused on Coopers Ferry and the Whitall family of Woodbury and Redbank. Grant GA-2287-17-001, to the Camden County Historical Society, funded our study of the Gloucester battlefield. Our profound thanks to the American Battlefield Protection Program staff, especially Kristen McMasters, Mattea Sanders, and Philip Bailey. Jack O'Byrne, Camden County Historical Society executive director, provided administrative support that sometimes stretched beyond his working hours.

Chapters 2 through 4 are condensed from portions of a future book on the American Revolution in South Jersey by Garry Stone. Our success in reconstructing the 1777 Town of Gloucester is due in large part to the late David C. Munn's exhaustive research into its people and places.

Our thanks to the staff of Westholme Publishing for seeing our words into print. Copy editor Ron Silverman ensured that text and notes conformed to the *Chicago Manual of Style*. Our particular thanks to series editor Mark Edward Lender. This book was his idea, and he shepherded drafts on their two-year trek to completion.

Index